RSAC DEC 1992

PLEASE RETURN THIS ITEM
BY THE DUE DATE TO ANY
TULSA CITY-COUNTY LIBRARY.

FINES A⸱ ⸱5¢ PER DAY; A
MAXIMUM O⸱ ⸱ ⸱ ⸱ PER ITEM.

D1573318

50,00
60B

Art from the Trenches

TEXAS A&M UNIVERSITY
20
MILITARY HISTORY SERIES

Art

from the Trenches

AMERICA'S UNIFORMED ARTISTS IN WORLD WAR I

By Alfred Emile Cornebise

TEXAS A&M UNIVERSITY PRESS · COLLEGE STATION

Copyright © 1991 by Alfred Emile Cornebise
Manufactured in the United States of America
All rights reserved
First Edition

Frontispiece: The Machine Gunner, H. T. Dunn, August, 1918, charcoal and watercolor
(*Smithsonian Institution*)

The paper used in this book meets the minimum requirements of the American National Standard
for Permanence of Paper for Printed Library Materials, Z39.48-1984. Binding materials have been chosen for durability. ⊗

Library of Congress Cataloging-in-Publication Data

Cornebise, Alfred E.
  Art from the trenches : America's uniformed artists in World War I
/ by Alfred Emile Cornebise. — 1st ed.
    p. cm. — (Texas A&M University military history series ; no.
20)
  Includes bibliographical references (p.) and index.
  ISBN 0-89096-349-5 (cloth)
  1. Art, American. 2. Art, Modern—20th century—United States.
3. World War, 1914–1918—Art and the war. I. Title. II. Series:
Texas A&M University military history series ; 20.
N6512.C598 1991
758′.99404′0973—dc20   90-23921
                        CIP

758.994040973 C814ar
1991
Cornebise, Alfred E.
Art from the trenches :

Contents

TULSA CITY-COUNTY LIBRARY

Preface

"When a war poses for its picture . . . it will sit with hands folded for those who wish it to, or it will strut with clanking sword, or pose as a mother of mercy, or the invading barbarian, or the valiant hero, or the cringing coward, or, better yet, a composite of all of these enveloped in a fury of sound and sight and horror."[1] With these words, Jules ("Jay") André Smith, one of eight official artists of the American Expeditionary Forces (AEF), suggests that the face of World War I presented countless opportunities—and difficulties—for anyone bent upon painting its likeness.

Building upon a long history of military and combat art, artists of the combatant nations set out to paint portraits of the struggle. Some were motivated to produce pure art using the plentiful dramatic subjects that the war provided. Others used their brushes and pens to produce propaganda pieces such as political cartoons. Still others produced recruiting posters urging citizens to enroll in national war efforts. Many other uses, such as camouflage, were found for art during the war years. Art was indeed a significant part of the scene by the time America entered its first war of the twentieth century. One art critic, Adeline Adams, was certain that American artists must participate in recording events: ". . . it *must* be told, the pictured story of our country's part in the World War," she insisted. This was all the more desirable, she continued, because "we, of all the peoples on earth, are the children of hope rather than of memory. We are of forward-looking habit; we have such a wealth of tomorrows on our mind that we forget our yesterdays, their glory and bitter cost." The men who served along the battlelines would not forget, "but what of the untouched homekeeping ones, and their children's children?" For their sakes, she concluded, "it is for us . . . to become the complete historians of the American boys at Château-Thierry, in the Argonne, at St. Mihiel, setting their story beside that of the heroes of Fredericksburg, Vicksburg, Gettysburg, and sparing no effort. . . ."2

The War Department had anticipated such needs by commissioning eight men as captains in the U.S. Army Corps of Engineers, designating them official artists of the AEF. They were William James Aylward, Walter Jack Duncan, Harvey Thomas Dunn, George M. Harding, Wallace Morgan, Ernest Clifford Peixotto, J. André Smith, and Harry Everett Townsend. Without much ado and, except for Smith, with no military training, from early 1918 until months after the Armistice these men were in France, and later Germany, performing their artistic duties. Not without controversy and beset by numerous difficulties that were a part of wartime service in a largely inexperienced army, they have left an artistic heritage worthy of serious consideration, study, appreciation, and enjoyment for the sake of the often striking art which much of it is.

This book is about artists and their role in wartime. In an introduction, I trace the history of battle art in the western world and the uses of art in the new type of war brought about by twentieth-century technology and conditions. My broad focus is on artists and their contributions to the war effort in 1914–1918. My narrow focus on the eight artists of the American Expeditionary Forces provides a case study of how official artists were chosen, how they worked, what they produced, how their work was received and used, and what place it occupied in the history of military art. Additional chapters detail the later careers of the artists and what became of their art. The pictures included in this book were selected to demonstrate the wide range of subjects and treatment of wartime themes by the AEF artists, long forgotten in the annals of American military and art history.

Acknowledgments

Numerous people have come to my aid in the preparation of this study. The Graduate School of the University of Northern Colorado, through its faculty assistance program, has made funds available to purchase many of the photographs used in the book and to help defray some travel expenses. Also at UNC, Lucy Schweers, and the staff in the Interlibrary Loan Office, have been unfailingly helpful to me in the long search for books and articles which they supplied in a virtually unending stream.

At the New Britain Museum of American Art in New Britain, Connecticut, Daniel DuBois, director; Lois L. Blomstrann, administration manager; and Jane Darnell, researcher, all aided me greatly in obtaining materials and information pertaining to Harry Townsend. Joan G. Robidoux, librarian at Lockwood House in Norwalk, Connecticut, helped me to find other sources relating to Townsend. By letter and phone, Walt Reed, of South Norwalk, Connecticut — illustrator, author, and historian, and an acknowledged expert on American illustrators — gave me much vital information on several artists, notably Townsend.

At the South Dakota Memorial Art Center, in Brookings, I received a most cordial welcome and much assistance from Joseph M. Stuart, director; Elaine Hietbrink, executive secretary; and Shelia Agee, assistant to the director. My study of Dunn has been greatly enhanced by their efforts.

Donald E. Kloster, curator, and Daniel P. Stanton, museum specialist, and the rest of the staff at the Division of Military History of the Smithsonian Institution's National Museum of American History have given me considerable help, advice, and encouragement. At the Division of Naval History, Frances Hainer diligently located the thirty-one pieces of AEF art that are housed there and not only made them available for my viewing but also arranged to have some photographed.

The indispensable person at the U.S. Army Center of Military History regarding military art is Mary Lou Gjernes, army art curator, who allowed me to view reproductions of their now considerable holdings of World War I art and directed me to further sources that proved most helpful.

The staff of the library at the National Portrait Gallery in Washington, D.C., and at the Archives of American Art, and also Christine Hennessey, assistant to the coordinator, Office of Research Support, Inventory of American Paintings, all advanced my efforts.

Cheryl Leibold, archivist at the Pennsylvania Academy of the Fine Arts, Philadelphia, gave me help in locating materials relating to many of the artists, especially George M. Harding. Also in Philadelphia, at the Free Library there, Marianne Promos provided me with useful information on several of the artists, again mainly on Harding. George M. Harding, Jr., of Wynnewood, Pennsylvania, also contributed useful facts about his father.

Julie Long, program coordinator at the Maitland Art Center, Maitland, Florida, gave me much help in developing the biography of J. André Smith, as did Dusty Gres, director of library services at the Maitland Public Library.

Stuart L. Butler, of the Navy and Old Army Branch, Military Archives Division, the National Archives, expedited the microfilming of Entry 224 in Record Group 120 for my use. The Still Pictures Branch at the archives also promptly filled my order for numerous photographs of the art and the artists. Both the Smithsonian Institution and the U.S. Army, as well as the National Archives, are to be thanked for permission to reproduce the illustrations in this study.

Jean Ashton, at the New-York Historical Society, provided me with useful information regarding Peixotto. Frederic B. Taraba, assistant to the director and librarian-archivist at the Society of Illustrators' library in New York City, proved a gracious host and wellspring of much information on the artists who had been most active in the society, particularly Dunn, Morgan, and Townsend.

John Marcham, editor of the *Cornell Alumni News*, found useful data on Smith and supplied me with relevant materials.

The usual caveat applies: None of the persons mentioned is responsible for my conclusions, the manner in which I have presented the subject, and certainly not for any errors.

Part I. Art and the Great War

1. Introduction

"Art and war are old companions," one art historian has asserted, further observing that "battlefields and soldiers have been popular subjects with artists since earliest times."[1] And so they have. The reasons are not hard to find. Although war has its uncounted tragedies and late in the twentieth century confronts humanity with cataclysmic dangers, fields of battle are charged with action, color, and dynamism that cannot fail to appeal to those with creative talent. John Trumbull, an American artist of the Revolutionary War era, revealed something of this appeal as he observed the Battle of Bunker Hill from Roxbury, being plainly fascinated by "the roar of artillery, the burst of shells (whose track, like that of a comet was marked on the dark sky by a long trail of light from the burning fuse)—and the blazing ruins of the town—[which] formed altogether a sublime scene of military magnificence and ruin."[2] Later, in World War I, the British portrait painter Ambrose McEvoy, engaged as a battle artist by the Canadians, found the battlefield to be "the most thrilling sight I have ever seen," and William Orpen, the British war artist of the same conflict, once exclaimed that in the war he had come "up against the biggest thing I have or ever can cross—in this world."[3]

Yet there is another side to it, as one scholar has stated: "War and art do not live easily together. Art is essentially one of the benefits of peace, when men's minds and spirits turn to the civilizing pleasures of reflection. Mankind tends to be sententious about war."[4]

Whether war is repulsive or attractive, the fact remains that since humans first went to battle, their conflicts have attracted artists, and few are the great painters who have not found war a viable subject or source of inspiration. For some, there was the need to develop themes that taught moral lessons (e.g., "War is evil"). Others, commissioned to glorify the deeds of some great commander, simply performed as professionals making a living. Patriotism stirred yet others, as did hero worship, and where these factors were present, propaganda was often not far behind. Some artists, especially in the Renaissance, wishing to distance themselves from the horrors of war and its violent human passions, had recourse to allegory, usually classical, or chose subjects from antiquity to comment on current events. Artists with a technical bent often focused on the machinery of warfare, providing military and naval historians of a later time with much useful information. The Bayeux Tapestry of the era of the Norman Conquest is a good example. Still others have provided vast panoramas illustrating tactics and strategy and providing additional information together with the graphic images of larger scenes of combat. Some painters focused on the impact of war on the innocent bystanders—the civilians—or the stricken individual soldier. Whether working on the large canvas or in a much smaller scope, the artist has therefore been drawn to the last extreme of human conflict—armed battle—and whether in the large view or the small, and for whatever reason, has sought to interpret war's shattering impact on human beings and their environment.

The invention of the camera by Joseph Nicéphore Niepce in 1826 and its perfection by Louis Jacques Mandé Daguerre and others brought a new dimension to the recording of war. The camera forced artists to reexamine their art and its role in recording battles, though the artist was not generally regarded as superfluous.

By the end of the nineteenth century, Europe had a long tradition of battle art which would be continued, often with striking results, in recording the wars of the twentieth century.

There is also a custom of military art in American history. As one scholar has correctly observed: "Until the twentieth century, in the United States military art was the independent activity of a disparate group of courageous and industrious individuals." Although this was the case, "the U.S. Army has fostered art by permitting both soldier and civilian artists to accompany troops and make sketches as the spirit moved them."[5] More often than not, American battle art emphasized nationalism and patriotism, with propaganda being ever-present. This is not surprising when one considers that the new United States was forged in conflict, needing to establish itself in the midst of grave dangers, and gain the people's support. A good example of propaganda art was the scene recorded by Paul Revere in a 1770 engraving, *The Bloody Massacre Perpetrated in King Street, Boston, 1770, on 5 March, by a Party of the 29 Regiment.*

Once the Revolutionary War came, numerous artists, many of whom were participants in combat, recorded its events. These included Col. John Trumbull, who served for a time as aide-de-camp on General Washington's staff, the portrait painter Charles Willson Peale, and others.[6]

The War of 1812 did not lack illustrators, and that struggle's naval action was especially well commemorated. The war with Mexico (1846–48) was also recorded, mainly in the medium of lithography, by then the preeminent form of popular illustration.[7] The Civil War produced several notable artists, and although a few daguerreotypes were made during the Mexican War, they were little known, and it was not until the Civil War that photographs were used extensively to record all aspects of military and naval life and action. Those of Mathew B. Brady and his many assistants are best known.[8] The popular magazines such as *Harper's Weekly* and *Frank Leslie's Illustrated Newspaper* included significant work such as the paintings of Winslow Homer and the cartoons of Thomas Nast, which brought the war into the nation's living rooms. In addition, the firm of Currier & Ives, founded in 1857 by James Merritt Ives and Nathaniel Currier, widely circulated their lithographs during the war. In this way, their names became familiar on the American cultural scene. To be sure, the Currier & Ives prints were not a photographer's record of events. The battle formations represented were as regular as those on parade. Battle lines were much too close together, and perspective was distorted as well. Although the realities of battle were lacking in these pictures, something of the ambiance and spirit of the struggle emerges, suggesting how art would always have a place in conveying to the viewer the essential nature of war, even after the arrival of the camera. Photography was perhaps too realistic and static, and though capable of evoking the deepest human feelings and emotions, artists would ultimately remain supreme in this respect and would always have their champions among those seeking to include painters among combatants in war.

In the years following the Civil War, the U.S. Army resumed its actions against the Indians, faithfully accompanied by many artists. The best known included Frederic Remington and Theodore R. Davis of *Harper's*.[9] The Spanish-American War in 1898 was "a golden moment for war correspondents, artists, and photographers," though the art was considerably better than the photography.[10]

With the ending of the Spanish-American War and the dawning of the twentieth century, far-reaching changes developed in warfare and in the corresponding need of battle artists to accommodate them. Total war meant the increased involvement and victimizing of civilians. The home front was increasingly a legitimate subject for combat art and civilians also were the intended audience of propaganda posters and cartoons in newspapers, magazines, and other publications. Also, the rank and file figured more heavily by virtue of their numbers in the mass armies. War was now increasingly waged by machines and explosives in incredible quantities, the result being far removed from the pageantry and splendor of the picturesque, open warfare of the Napoleonic era.[11] As one critic noted: "Hell is no longer the color it used to be." In place of the brilliant palls of smoke, the dash of cavalry, and the lurid glare of the sky, there was widespread use of smokeless powder, and a vast destruction. A general bleakness prevailed, yet alive with fateful forces and "earth-colored troops, like bits of earth, made living men." While World War I landscapes sometimes possessed their own haunting beauty and epic quality, "among shapely shadowed ruins," which could be reproduced in color, the viewer had to forgo the battle picture of the nineteenth century, with its striking shades and its melodramatic scenes.[12] The ruins and blighted landscapes required a new art to do it justice. The emphasis was on greater realism, a preoccupation to which the refinement and widespread use of photography contributed. The artist had to compete with the camera's ability to reveal the horrors of war in stark reality. That artists succeeded is attested to by combat art's survival to the present day.

Despite the traditions of war art, World War I was the first war in which systematic and copious use was made of artists and their talents. For instance, artists were entrusted with organizing the camouflage activities of the armies and navies, the art of deception being a great preoccupation in this conflict. As is true with many innovations and inventions, the origins of camouflage are obscure. The French, however, assign credit for its invention to the painter Victor Lucien Guirand de Scevola, who stated that he formed the idea of dissimulating war machinery by employing Cubist techniques.[13] Whatever its origins, soon after the Battle of the Marne in September of 1914, the French High Command ordered camouflage sections established within the Corps of Engineers. By the war's end, more than three thousand French artists of all ages and artistic schools had served the nation in this capacity. The Germans rapidly established similar units, followed by the British, who naturally gave considerable attention to marine camouflage, which, with the development of the submarine threat, gave specific focus to their efforts. Even the Americans did some early work in the field.

In the new era of the citizen army, with its need for huge amounts of money and millions of people, numerous other artists were employed to paint posters appealing for the enlistment of both lives and treasure. Cartoonists became powerful molders of public opinion, and no self-respecting newspaper or magazine ignored them.[14] But as in other wars, the most dramatic art was that produced by artists who, shunning the dangers and their peaceful studios, took their talents and their sketchpads directly onto the battlefield.

The British, Canadians, and Australians were among the first to recognize the value of war art in the new conflict, although official programs took some time to develop. When the war began, the British artists flocked to the colors in great numbers.[15] Thirty, for example, joined the Medical Corps en masse; others joined the special regiment for intellectuals and artists, the "Artists' Rifles." Some were engaged in camouflage work. All seemed caught up in the general euphoria of the times, the initial excitement that would later wear exceedingly thin. Many desired active service for professional reasons, seeing it as vital to their growth as artists. The British Vorticist painter Percy Wyndham Lewis wrote, "You must not miss a war if one is going! You cannot afford to miss that experience." Indeed, for Christopher Richard Wynne Nevinson, the British Futurist artist, war was the supreme stimulus: "There is no beauty except in strife, no masterpiece without aggressiveness."[16] The results of the early experiences of such painters were works of art that attracted public attention through exhibitions and publication in magazines and newspapers.

It was not until the war had worn on that it was decided officially to use artists in some systematic way to record the war effort and scenes of battle. As early as August of 1914, to be sure, the British cabinet had created a propaganda department located at Wellington House, in London. This organization was concerned with developing propaganda materials, especially books and pamphlets, for wide circulation, to counter German efforts. But subsequently, the need arose for materials of a pictorial nature to supplement the photographic record. The decision was made to employ the best available artists to produce the desired works. In this way, the British created high quality battle art, particularly during the last two years of the conflict. The results impressed American art critic Albert Eugene Gallatin, who stated that, as a result of their programs, the British had emerged with "a very adequate pictorial record of the Great War, a record which far outstrips that of any other country, Canada only excepted." Even France was left behind, he concluded, and the United States was "nowhere at all." In short, the British created collections of which "the British nation may congratulate itself upon owning."[17]

But the French did employ official artists, in addition to those engaged in camouflage work. However, many of France's large art colony dutifully went to the front to fight. Some, too old for combat, entered industry, laying aside their art for the duration, though some continued to paint when conditions permitted. Their work fell generally into two categories: the relatively few propagandistic works and the far more numerous sketches of life in the trenches and garrisions. Much of this art was published in popular magazines and newspapers and in such wartime journals as *L'Élan*, and *La Crapouillot*.[18] Later the French minister of war ordered the creation of a group of artist-painters, whose duty it was to paint action pictures "so as to immortalize on canvas true pictures of fighting in the field."[19] Some of this art toured America, the French hoping to influence American opinion to support the Allies.[20] Among the accomplishments of French artists was the creation and wide circulation of poster art. Concerned with all aspects of the war, the home front as well as combat zones, French posters remain a significant part of the war's artistic legacy.[21]

The immense quantity and impressive quality of war art in the Allied countries encouraged Americans to create their own. This they did almost as soon as America entered the war, on April 6, 1917. Artists immediately volunteered their brushes and pencils as weapons in the struggle. Many offered their services to the government free of charge. Some called themselves "Artists for Victory"; others, from the Society of Illustrators, were known as the "Vigilantes." The latter group was headed by Charles Dana Gibson, the illustrator who had created the popular "Gibson Girl."[22] He and many like him were soon put to work by George Creel, head of the newly created Committee on Public Information. This committee was charged with coordinating propaganda, both domestic and foreign, on behalf of the war effort. Creel at once recognized the importance of pictorial publicity, especially posters, "in building morale, arousing the spiritual forces of the Nation, and stimulating the will of the people."[23]

To these ends, and to produce other forms of art, on April 17, 1917, the Division of Pictorial Publicity of the Committee on Public Information was established, with Gibson as chairman. From his New York offices he began to coordinate much of the official artistic endeavor. As the work rapidly expanded, it became necessary to establish branch offices in Chicago, Boston, and San Francisco. Soon painters, sculptors, designers, illustrators, and cartoonists throughout the country were involved. Contacts were made with various branches of government to determine poster and publicity needs. By the end of the war, 1,438 pieces of work had been produced for fifty-eight agencies. Much of the work was done for the American Red Cross, for the Treasury and its several Liberty Loan drives, and for the Shipping Board, which was seeking workers for the shipyards.[24] Many of these posters possessed considerable persuasive power, as did one by A. E. Foringer that described the Red Cross as the "Greatest Mother in the World." The image subsequently became the symbol of that agency to the end of the war. Certainly one of the best known of the recruiting posters created for the U.S. Army was by James Montgomery Flagg. His "I Want You" poster with the famous pointing finger of Uncle Sam borrowed the pose from the earlier British creation by Alfred Leete that featured Lord Kitchener demanding recruits for the British army. Other work accomplished included large paintings intended to solicit support for Liberty Loans or other campaigns. These large outdoor paintings, displayed in front of public buildings, attracted crowds of onlookers.[25]

Much was done by artists outside the Division of Pictorial Publicity. The U.S. Navy had its own organization for pictorial publicity. Under its direction,

Henry Reuterdahl, Howard Chandler Christy, and Flagg produced numerous striking works.[26] Gibson painted posters for the United States Shipping Board Emergency Fleet Corporation, which urged a speedup of ship construction, one of the dire needs of the time.

Not all artists in America interested in supporting the war effort worked under government direction. Some of the best art was produced independently. Joseph Pennell and Vernon Howe Bailey created numerous lithographs and drawings, and painted scenes from various war industries in America.[27] Among the prominent artists who contributed to the flood of art on the war theme were George Bellows, George Luks, Augustus Vincent Tack, and Childe Hassam.

Once at war, America shared other nations' concern with camouflage. Maj. Evarts Tracy, an architect, was charged with creating the initial camouflage unit in the U.S. Army in August of 1917. Attached to the Corps of Engineers, it was stationed at American University in Washington, D.C. Ordered to the detachment were artists, architects, ornamental iron workers, tinsmiths, plasterers, photographers, and stage carpenters. Eventually several schools of camouflage were established, all requiring staffs of skilled artists. In the navy, camouflage schemes were worked out by the Navy Department, but their actual execution was accomplished by the United States Shipping Board Emergency Fleet Corporation's department of camouflage, which stationed a camoufleur in each of its districts with a corps of trained men under his orders.[28]

Other artists painted "landscape" or "designation targets" for use in training camps.[29] Yet others were employed in constructing masks to cover facial injuries suffered by many troops in combat.[30] Sculptors created medals for use by the army and navy and by civilian agencies.[31] Architects found employment in the Department of Labor's Bureau of Industrial Housing and Transportation, creating housing for workers. Entire towns were built to support the rapidly burgeoning war industries. Others obtained commissions in the Engineer Corps and were set to work designing buildings, bases, port facilities, and air fields.

Other decorative work created by artists included the Victory Arch, a temporary plaster structure erected in New York City at Madison Square and Fifth Avenue to honor New York's returning troops after the war. An impressive Victory Way was erected on Park Avenue and consisted of rows of Doric columns. It featured a frieze of paintings honoring various Allied nations.[32] Along Fifth Avenue, dozens of prominent store windows became the settings for works of patriotic art.[33]

It was against the background of this varied and often intense artistic activity that artists went to the war zone in France. Several of those who made the journey did not hold official positions. These unofficial artists included Samuel Johnson Woolf, Will Foster, and Lester G. Hornby, some of whose art appeared in such magazines as *Scribner's* and *Harper's*. Jo Davidson and Robert I. Aitken modeled busts of Allied generals and statesmen. Joseph Cummings Chase went to France in 1919 to paint the portraits of various American and Allied officers and enlisted men who had been decorated with the nation's highest honors: the Medal of Honor, the Distinguished Service Cross, or the Distinguished Service Medal. Louis Orr, later a popular cartoonist for the *Chicago Tribune,* produced some striking etchings of Rheims Cathedral under fire.[34]

Several men who served in the armed forces produced some interesting battle art. These included the black artist, George Picken; Horace Pippin; Henry Schnakenberg, of the U.S. Army Medical Corps; and Thomas Benton and Louis Bouche, of the Navy. Henry Varnum Poor worked as a regimental artist, and Kerr Eby, sometimes mistakenly identified as an official artist, painted many works while serving as an enlisted man in the Corps of Engineers.[35]

Though war art was being produced by many artists using varied media and techniques, only eight men were officially charged with the responsibility of producing art for the AEF. These men joined together in a common cause: to create a pictorial memoir of the war.

2. The Army's Official Artists

The first suggestion for the appointment of official artists by the U.S. government for special service with the American Expeditionary Forces, then assembling in Europe, was apparently made by Kendall Banning in July of 1917.[1] Banning, in charge of photographs and films for the Division of Films under Creel's Committee on Public Information, consulted with representatives of Great Britain and France, who advised him that capable artists should be commissioned and assigned to duty within military zones not open to civilians.[2] Though several artists were approached, by the end of 1917 no progress had been made in their selection, and the Committee on Public Information was no longer being considered as the agency to supervise them. The Signal Corps of the U.S. Army then took up the idea, but its plans came to nothing at first, although they were later successful.

In December of 1917, Capt. Aymar Embury II, of the Engineer Reserve Corps, himself an artist, asked Maj. Gen. William M. Black, chief of the Army Corps of Engineers, if it would be possible for the Engineers to take up the plan, as apparently the Signal Corps was not going to proceed. General Black, convinced of the merits of the scheme, sought and obtained consent from the War Department to launch the program. Embury was then instructed to submit the names of four painters who might be likely candidates. Before anything could be arranged, however, Gen. John J. Pershing, commander-in-chief of the American Expeditionary Forces, was consulted on the matter. He agreed that such appointments would be desirable and asked that the four be sent abroad immediately. In the meantime, the Signal Corps, reconsidering the possibilities, independently approached Pershing and also asked for the commissioning of four artists working under Signal Corps direction. Agreeing to this request, Pershing wired Washington that he would accept four additional men. To avoid confusion, however, it was decided that all of the men would be commissioned as captains in the Engineer Reserve Corps.

Candidates were selected from two lists. One list contained the four names submitted by General Black. A second list of twelve names was drawn up by Charles Dana Gibson, chairman of the Pictorial Publicity Committee of Creel's Committee on Public Information, and members of that committee.[3] In early February, 1918, J. André Smith (already a first lieutenant in the Engineers), Kendall Banning (by then a major in the Signal Reserve Corps), Col. James G. Steese of the Corps of Engineers, and Gibson met in Steese's Washington office to pick the final eight names. General Black's list of four was accepted, although only Harvey Dunn and Smith of the four subsequently accepted the offer. Ernest Peixotto was the third man selected. His appointment was recommended by well-known sculptor Herbert Adams, warmly seconded by Gibson, and finalized in a personal interview with Colonel Steese. The five remaining artists were chosen from the list submitted by Gibson's committee. These were William James Aylward, Walter Jack Duncan, George M. Harding, Wallace Morgan, and Harry Everett Townsend. Probably because of Gibson's influence, six of the men were mainly magazine and book illustrators (Aylward, Duncan, Dunn, Harding, Morgan, and Townsend). Peixotto, described as a "nearly pure artist," and Smith, an architect who was also an etcher of some repute, were the exceptions.[4] Although the artists worked mainly as illustrators, they came from widely diverse backgrounds.

Capt. Aylward

NATIONAL ARCHIVES

William James Aylward was born in Milwaukee on September 5, 1875, to a Great Lakes shipowner. Aylward's early contact with ships was to have great influence on his later artistic career. He once observed: "As my father was a ship-builder . . . and vessel-owner in a small way, sailing his own schooner on the Great Lakes, I naturally inclined toward 'sea-stuff.'"[5]

Aylward attended St. John's Cathedral School in Milwaukee, later studying at the Art Institute of Chicago, the Art Students' League in New York City, and then with the famous American illustrator-teacher, Howard Pyle, who maintained studios at Chadds Ford, Pennsylvania, near Philadelphia, and at Wilmington, Delaware. Pyle instructed a surprisingly large number of first-rate illustrators, including five of the eight official artists of the AEF.[6] Aylward completed his training in Europe, studying privately with several artists.

After his art training, Aylward began his career as an illustrator and writer. Appearing in *Scribner's Magazine* and *Harper's*, much of his work dealt with English naval life in the eighteenth century and the age of the clipper ships. He also illustrated books, such as Jack London's *Sea Wolf* (1904), Jules Verne's *Twenty Thousand Leagues under the Sea* (1925), and other works on naval or marine subjects.[7]

Aylward was perhaps best known, however, for his advertising art, a form which rapidly developed and matured in the United States in the early twentieth century. He produced many advertisements for steamship companies and other firms desiring to feature the sea in their ads. Aylward once remarked that advertising was "also a means of educating public taste for better art, as it is scattered broadcast in our publications from coast to coast, and [which] . . . must finally have a *good* effect. It has been discovered that good art pays the advertiser."[8]

In an age in which an artist or writer was expected to develop one area of expertise, Aylward became quite versatile, producing architectural and figure subjects with the same facility that he displayed in his marine works. Nevertheless, the spirit of romance and adventure that was invariably associated with the sea permeated Aylward's best work. Recognizing this, *Scribner's* commissioned him to take an extended ocean trip. He began his journey at the Patuxent River, in Maryland, joining the U.S. Navy Dry Dock Flotilla, which was engaged in towing the dry dock, *Dewey*, to the Philippines. Aylward wrote and illustrated a lengthy article for *Scribner's* in which he narrated the adventures and misadventures of the trip.[9] From the Philippines, Aylward continued on to the Orient before returning to San Francisco in a four-masted sailing bark. He then spent several years in France, painting port scenes, while continuing to illustrate stories for *Harper's* and *Scribner's*. Back in the United States, he spent considerable time cruising with Gloucester and New York fishing vessels, eventually buying his own small boat, berthing it at Manhasset Bay, Long Island.[10]

Meanwhile, Aylward regularly exhibited his artwork, winning several prizes and awards. Among those he received were the Shaw Purchase Prize at the Salmagundi Club in 1911; the Beck Prize, of the Philadelphia Color Club, in 1912; and the Salmagundi Prize for Illustration in 1914.[11]

Aylward's credentials as an illustrator were clearly of the highest order. His familiarity with the world, including his considerable knowledge of France, no doubt contributed to his selection as one of the official artists of the AEF. He was duly commissioned on March 21, 1918, and soon reported for duty at Chaumont, France, headquarters of the AEF.[12]

Capt. Duncan

Walter Jack Duncan was born in Indianapolis on January 1, 1881, into a family prominent in theater circles. His grandfather, John Jack Duncan, was a renowned

Shakespearean actor. His mother, Rosalie Jack, was a member of the Reed family, also well known for several generations as thespians.

When he completed high school, Duncan and a school companion, Robert Cortes Holliday, who would gain some renown as a writer and artist, moved to New York City. There they shared the proverbial garret while studying art at the Art Students' League. The boys became pupils of John H. Twachtman, a "brusque little man with graying bangs and a mephistophelian manner, whom his fellow artists pronounced the greatest of American landscape artists."[13] Duncan remained at the league from 1899 to 1902. It was by then a well-known institution with four hundred students and the best art instructors in the country. If the well-heeled art students sailed to the mecca of art at the turn of the century—Paris—and its Atelier Julien and École des Beaux-Arts, many aspiring American artists had to settle for the Art Students' League. Nevertheless, they received first-rate instruction in a place that featured "a guild spirit, being co-operatively run and managed by its students," and an artistic atmosphere all its own. Some of the prominent men who served as instructors at that time were Kenyon Cox, William Merritt Chase, Thomas Eakins, and Edwin H. Blashfield. Among its students who gained prominence were Howard Pyle, George Inness, Rufus Fairchild Zogbaum, Thoré de Thulstrup, and Charles Dana Gibson. For a brief time, Frederic Remington studied there as well.

Like many budding illustrators, Duncan found the turn of the century a propitious time for the launching of his career, and in 1903 he established himself with the *Century Magazine.* Two years later, *Scribner's* sent him to England for a set of drawings, and in 1907 he became connected with *McClure's Magazine.* In 1912, he joined the staff of *Harper's,* which sent him to Canada on assignment and later to the Kentucky mountains, "where he drew the descendants of Daniel Boone and his pioneers living under the same conditions that their ancestors found when they first surged across the mountains."[14]

Duncan's specialty was pen and ink, "which he employed with great directness and skill, . . . [resulting] from his very careful and thoroughly worked out preliminary studies."[15] Indeed, pen drawing was his favorite medium, especially for book illustration, and he developed it to a high degree, being acknowledged as the "wizard of pen and ink." He once observed that "an illustration drawn in line with a pen and ink, and in the manner that types were originally designed, is, naturally enough, in perfect keeping with the text, and with it sparkles enchantingly against its sunny back-ground of white paper."[16]

Indeed, Duncan cared about books and writers and was closely associated with many authors, including Robert Holliday and Booth Tarkington. One of his favorite writers was Christopher Morley, and Duncan illustrated several of his books, including *Tales from a Rolltop Desk* (1921), *Plum Pudding* (1921), and *Pipefuls* (1927). One critic wrote, "Duncan, with his mastery of line and fecund imagination, visualizes as if they were a part of his own experience Morley's city squares and railway stations, docks and country lanes, his wistful dogs, his fishermen, and all the company that throng his pages."[17] He would soon turn these talents to military subjects.

The later artistic career of Harvey Thomas Dunn was one of considerable attainment both as teacher and artist, and his experiences in the war influenced his later career to a substantial degree. He carried with him deep impressions of the conflict and continued to produce battlefield scenes long after he had left them behind and most of the other official artists had ceased painting them.

More has been written about Dunn than any of the other artists, and he has been the subject of two biographies, though both are by the same author.[18] Dunn's father, William Thomas Dunn, took up a homestead three miles south of Manchester, Dakota Territory, having moved from Wisconsin with his wife, Bersha Dow Dunn. Harvey, born March 8, 1884, was the second of the three children in the family. William Thomas Dunn sold his original homestead in 1888 and moved a few miles away to another farm, where Harvey grew up. The Dunn children attended the one-room rural school of Esmond Township, and Harvey's first art endeavors were sketchings on the school's blackboard. Harvey was large for his age—over six feet tall at fourteen—but as with most farm lads, he was already doing a man's hard farm labor. But his inclinations turned toward art early on, and with his mother's encouragement he enrolled at South Dakota Agricultural College (later South Dakota State University) at Brookings in 1901. Under the influence of an art professor, Ada Berthan Caldwell, Harvey was encouraged to leave college and pursue his art studies at the Art Institute of Chicago. Although his career at Chicago was not auspicious, he no doubt matured as an artist. To further his development, Dunn applied to work with renowned artist-teacher Howard Pyle, of Wilmington, Delaware. Having found his mentor at last, Dunn made rapid progress. While studying with Pyle, Dunn encountered many artists, including future AEF artists William J. Aylward and Ernest Peixotto.[19] Dunn also met his bride-to-be in Wilmington, Johanne Louise ("Tulla") Krebs, the daughter of a prominent local businessman.

After studying with Pyle for two years, from 1904 to 1906, Dunn established his own studio in Wilmington to launch his career as an illustrator and teacher.

Capt. Dunn

National Archives

His timing was opportune, because weekly and monthly periodicals were clamoring for competent artists' work, to use for illustrating stories and in advertising. Book publishers also drew heavily upon illustrators' skills, and Dunn began busily illustrating the novels of such writers as E. W. Hornung, Rex Beach, Jack London, and many others.[20]

Periodicals, such as *Outing,* also purchased Dunn's work, although the longest lasting professional relationship Dunn established was with the *Saturday Evening Post,* extending from 1906 to 1939. Dunn illustrated stories by William Allen White, Irvin S. Cobb, Kathleen Norris, Rudyard Kipling, and others for this magazine.

In 1914, for proximity to the New York art markets, Dunn moved with his wife and two children to Leonia, New Jersey, across the Hudson from the Bronx. In the following year, he and Charles Shepard Chapman founded the Leonia School of Illustration, hoping to carry on the traditions of Pyle, who had died in Florence, Italy, in 1911. However, Dunn and Chapman did not work well together and gave up the school just prior to America's entry into World War I. Nevertheless, Dunn had proved himself an able teacher, attracting to the school such artists and illustrators of later note as Frank Street, Harry Ballinger, William Cameron Menzies, Arthur Mitchell, and perhaps his best student of those days, Dean Cornwell. Then, selected as an official artist for the AEF, Dunn was commissioned on March 7, 1918, just one day before his thirty-fourth birthday. He formally entered the army at Camp Merritt, near Tenafly, New Jersey, and was soon on his way to war.

Capt. Harding

NATIONAL ARCHIVES

During World War II, a seaman in the American light cruiser U.S.S. *Montpelier* recorded in his diary one day, as the ship steamed northward to cover the landing of the troops on the Pacific island of Emirau, that "we have an old Marine Captain on board for the trip. He does a lot of painting. He's painted pictures of the ships in our group as we sail along. He has also painted different parts of the ship as the guns, mounts, turrets, etc."[21] The "old Marine Captain" was surely George Harding, who served as an official artist in both world wars: in the first as a captain in the U.S. Army Corps of Engineers and in the second as a captain of Marines.

Born on October 2, 1882, in Philadelphia, George Matthews Harding became interested in art early in his life as he observed his older sister's developing artistic career. Charlotte Harding, nine years older than her brother, studied art at the Philadelphia School of Design for Women, the Pennsylvania Academy of the Fine Arts, and, as so many other artists had, with Howard Pyle, then at the Drexel Institute in Philadelphia. Encouraged by his sister, George Harding first studied architecture for a brief time at Boston Tech and then art at the Pennsylvania Academy of the Fine Arts, taking classes at night while working by day as an architect in the offices of Frederich Mann in Philadelphia. Introduced by his sister to Howard Pyle, George subsequently studied with him at his studio at Chadds Ford and in Wilmington.[22]

In 1903, following the conclusion of his art education, Harding's first illustrations appeared in the *Saturday Evening Post*, where as Harding later explained it, the editor, George Lorimer, "took youngsters at twenty-one and gave them stories to illustrate."[23]

In 1906, Harding joined the staff of *Harper's Monthly Magazine*, which sent him to Newfoundland and Labrador. There he wrote and illustrated articles about the lives of the captains and crews of sealing and fishing ships, during the course of which he himself suffered shipwreck, an event he wrote about for the magazine. There followed trips in hurricane season with marine surveyors engaged in salvaging cargo from storm-wrecked freighters in the West Indies.[24] While in the Caribbean, Harding in 1911 covered the first overseas airplane flight in the Western Hemisphere, from Key West to Havana. He was aboard one of the U.S. Navy destroyers stationed every fifteen miles out in the Gulf to rescue the airmen if they went down. He then went back to northern waters, living for a time at the lighthouse at Cape Race, Newfoundland. There he gathered material about shipboard use of communications and the dangers of icebergs, writing several articles, one of which, about ice in the shipping lanes, appeared in *Harper's* at the very time that the *Titanic* went down.[25]

Harding's success as an author-illustrator convinced *Harper's* to send him on a trip around the world, which lasted from 1912 to 1914. He visited Egypt, Arabia, India, Australia, the Dutch East Indies, the Malay States, China, and numerous South Sea islands. Traveling by stagecoach, on camel, and aboard sailing craft and cargo steamers, there "unfolded more than romantic prospects," he wrote.[26] Significantly for his artistic development, he encountered examples of Asian and Pacific art which greatly influenced him for the remainder of his life. During the process of assimilating what he had seen, however, he developed his own impressionistic style. This was coupled with the primitive, under the influence in particular of ancient Chinese frescoes, East Indian cave paintings, and the native art of the islands of the South Pacific. These disparate influences, rather than French Impressionism, led Harding to his own lack of concern with the literal shape of things and his incorporating of impressionistic abstract content into his art.[27] Harding's travels and his accumulation of first-hand impressions and material served as the basis for much future artistic work. During the trip he also illustrated books written by his traveling companion, prolific author Norman Duncan.[28]

Soon after his return to the United States, in 1915, Harding joined the fine arts department of the University of Pennsylvania. In the following year, he set up his own studio and launched a parallel career as a mural painter, decorating hotels, theaters, and other buildings. In 1916, he married Anita Cotheal Nisbett, in Ardmore, Pennsylvania, and they later had two children.[29]

Following America's entry into the war, Harding served on the poster committee of the U.S. Navy Recruiting Service. When the decision was made to commission eight AEF artists, Harding's travel experiences and his maturing career were known by members of the selection committee, especially Joseph Pennell, who, Harding once remarked, "strongly recommended my appointment." So, he concluded: "At thirty-four and with a lot of knocking about behind me, I found myself in the Army." He was soon at Hoboken and on board the transport, *Philadelphia*, bound for the conflict in France.[30]

Capt. Morgan

NATIONAL ARCHIVES

Wallace Morgan was born in New York City on July 11, 1873. His father, William Penn Morgan, was an art instructor and a painter. Soon after Wallace's birth, the family moved to Albany, New York, where he grew up. Following his high school years, he returned to New York City, intent upon becoming an artist. As he once recalled, "I thought little of illustration then and hoped to become a painter, particularly of murals and I dreamt of covering great walls with my designs."[31]

He began his studies at the National Academy of Design. In order to pay his way, he landed a part-time job as artist on the *New York Sun*. He remained at the *Sun* for a year, until in 1898 an opportunity came to join James Gordon Bennett's *New York Herald* as a member of the regular staff. In those days before the general use of photography and the halftone plate, newspapers depended on artists as they do on photographers today. Morgan covered daily assignments by going with the reporters and drawing pictures at the scene of events. He thus "went through the tough school of the newspaper artist. . . . Forced to draw a constant variety of subjects under pressure, on the spot or from memory, he emerged with such facility that he never needed models in his work. His finished renderings were attempted directly, without preliminary sketches."[32] In short, "the constant variety, the difficulties, and the excitement of having to race against time developed initiative, speed, accuracy, and keen powers of observation." Morgan therefore "possessed in a high degree the ability to inject life and action into an illustration, and he could convey to the average newspaper reader exactly the atmosphere of the scene which he pictured."[33]

He also developed a working philosophy, concluding that "after all, the illustrator should comment on life. We have the duty of showing up fraud and pomposity and to get across human frailty." All of these attributes prepared him for the rigorous service at the front later with the AEF, his quick sketching abilities being especially useful for recording life in the trenches.[34]

But that was in the future. Earlier in his career, Morgan attracted some attention for two ventures that he undertook. The first came when Mt. Pelée erupted on Martinique in May of 1902. With other journalists, he boarded a seagoing tug and headed for the Caribbean, arriving off the island a few days after the volcano's initial explosion. The second eruption soon occurred, and Morgan "sketched until his arm grew numb," producing some remarkable drawings of the event.[35]

Later, in 1907, the poet Carolyn Wells sent some verses about "a blonde little scatterbrain called Fluffy Ruffles" to the *Herald*. Morgan was given the assignment of illustrating the poems, which he did as color cartoons. Morgan, not knowing how to dress "Fluffy," "used to hurry into Brentano's for the latest French fashion magazines and copy the styles before Miss and Mrs. America had seen them," and he thereby became a setter of styles in women's apparel. "Funny thing," Morgan once remarked, "I put a little frilly jacket on her. The darned thing is still being worn. Also, I gave her low-heeled pumps, which the modern girls are still wearing. Odd how they've kept on."[36] So popular did she become that Charles Frohman produced a play about her, written by Clyde Fitch, and she became known internationally as an "American type of girl," a challenger of the earlier "Gibson Girl."

Morgan's success enabled him to terminate his position with the *Herald* after eleven years, and he set up his own studio, working thereafter on commissions. One of the most important of these came in 1914 when *Collier's* engaged him and his friend Julian Street to travel about America and report their findings "in prose and paint." Two books resulted, being first published serially in *Collier's* as "witty chapters in Americana."[37]

A third trip across America was interrupted by the country's entry into World War I and Morgan's selection as one of the official AEF artists. He was commissioned on March 1, 1918, and reported at Chaumont on April 1, one of the first of the eight to arrive in France.

NATIONAL ARCHIVES

Capt. Peixotto

The painter of the group who has been described as a "nearly pure artist," Ernest Clifford Peixotto, was born on October 15, 1869, into a prominent merchant family in San Francisco. He began his artistic career in his native city, studying under

Emil Carlsen at the School of Fine Arts at the Mark Hopkins Institute in 1886, remaining there until 1888. He then entered the Atelier Julien in Paris, and there and at the Ateliers de Peinture, Sculpteur, et Dessin he studied with Benjamin Constant, Jules Joseph Lefebvre, and Henri Lucien Doucet, staying three years in all.[38]

Beginning in 1890, and for several years to follow, he exhibited pictures at the Paris Salon; in 1895, one of his works, *A Woman of Rijsoord,* won an honorable mention. Thus, as he once expressed it, as a "mere boy" he encountered France and "the country and its picturesque towns and villages took a strong hold on me." Later, he spent several summers in Giverny, in Normandy, "and then, as well as since, . . . [I] have explored every nook of this pretty bit of countryside in all forms of conveyance—bicycle, motor car, and in an open carriage."[39]

Peixotto eventually became a member of the Yacht Club of France and, using its facilities, took extended motorboat cruises along the waterways of the nation, taking notes and sketching as he proceeded. The results of these ventures were published in his book, *Through the French Provinces,* which appeared in 1909. The account reveals the American sophisticate among the peasants, all of whom are depicted as simple, picturesque folk. In Paris, he was a habitué of the outdoor cafes, one of his favorites being the Pêche Miraculeuse along the Seine on the western edge of Paris. Thus, ever the close observer of France, its customs, and her people, Peixotto enjoyed a leisurely existence, experiencing to the full the pleasures of the Old World which "in its sunset was fair to see," as Winston Churchill once wrote.[40] Peixotto would later feel the changed situation in France all the more acutely.

For two years, Peixotto lived in New York City, working from 1897 to 1899 for *Scribner's* and *Harper's.* On January 28, 1897, he married Mary Glascock Hutchinson of New Orleans, who had also studied art with Emil Carlsen. Leaving America in 1899, Peixotto and his wife established a studio-home near Fontainebleau, at Samois-sur-Seine, which they used as a base of operations. Then, reflecting his Hispanic heritage (his grandfather had immigrated to the United States from Spain) Peixotto began to follow the "Hispanic Trail," visiting Spain, Portugal, Peru, Bolivia, and the American Southwest, writing articles and books, which he also illustrated.[41] During these years he also found time to illustrate books and articles written by others, and in 1911, he executed a group of large murals on the theme "La Mort d'Arthur" for the Cleveland Public Library. The boldness of his designs and their vivid coloring resulted in numerous commissions to paint decorations for rooms in Paris and New York City, and for villas in Italy, California, Florida, and elsewhere.[42]

In July of 1914, as war was about to break out, he and his wife had just returned to their studio from Portugal. All was quiet momentarily, but as soon as the posting of the Order of General Mobilization was made, great changes occurred, Peixotto noting that "dread and grief were already in the air." Five days later, he joined the local communal guard which "day or night, patrolled the roads, the fields, the woods, the river banks, watching for spies, for malefactors, for deserters, with orders to stop and question everyone. Those were agonizing days that lengthened into weeks, lightened at last by the Victory of the Marne."[43]

In October of 1914, Peixotto returned to America, trying to content himself by working on various projects. But he was restless, deploring the fact that his age prevented his entering active military service. Following America's entry into the war, his opportunity came at last, and in February of 1918, he was offered his captaincy as an official artist, which he took up with enthusiasm. He was thus able to bring his considerable experience as traveler, painter, and writer to the artistic effort assigned to him. Since he possessed an intimate knowledge of France and spoke the language fluently, he was ideally fitted for the work and could proceed without lost motion. On March 4, he received telegraphic notification of his appointment, and ten days later, he was on the *Pocahontas,* bound for France.

"When one first confronts the legacy of art left to the world by J. André Smith, . . . one's initial reaction is wonder and awe that one artist could create such a huge body of superb work in so many differing media." Thus an unknown critic could only marvel at the "hundreds of etchings, thousands of drawings, strong expressionist monotypes—reminiscent of Goya's late fantasies, [and] paper sculture [pieces]" of the architect and etcher of the AEF group. Even the most casual observer would certainly be awed by Smith's "scores of oils, watercolors, works in collage, and much more."[44]

The man who created it all was born in Hong Kong on December 31, 1880, only a few minutes before the new year. Smith's father was a sea captain and shipowner, and when Captain Smith, Sr., died at sea seven years after the future artist's birth, his family moved to Hamburg, Germany. The Smiths relocated to Boston in 1890 and finally settled permanently in New York City in 1893.[45]

Smith's interest in art dates to his public school days in Columbia Grammar School, and he did his first artwork at that time. Some success in these early ventures encouraged him to major in architecture at Cornell when he entered in 1898. In 1902 he was art editor of the *Cornellian,* the school's yearbook. Ever after closely interested in Cornell's affairs, he later helped to illustrate the *Cornell Alumni News,* and his ornate, classical cover for that publication was used from 1911 to 1933.

Capt. Smith

Smith graduated in 1902 with a degree in architecture. He spent the following months in an architect's office in New York, but in 1903, he returned to Cornell as a Resident Fellow in Architecture, receiving his master of science degree in that field in 1904. Smith received a Traveling Fellowship from Cornell for 1904–1906 that enabled him to continue his studies at various places in Europe. After his return, Smith worked for two years for a New York City architectural firm as draftsman and designer. But he preferred painting and etching to architecture and pursued these initially in his spare time.

Having developed considerable skill as an etcher, in 1910 Smith held exhibitions of his work in New York and later at Cornell. Encouraged by the response to his efforts, Smith changed careers in 1911, establishing himself as an etcher and painter. He developed the ability to work accurately and rapidly, which would serve him well on the battlefields of Europe. (Because of his speed, he created more pieces of art than any of his AEF colleagues.) He also learned how to draw on the copper plates direct from nature, without any preliminary "drawing-in." He liked to complete his work in a single sitting, "with the belief that one could not return to a subject and view it with the same spirit and enthusiasm as one does at first sight." He also did his own printing.[46]

Despite his successes, Smith decided to return to Europe, seeking to develop further as an artist. He produced many etchings of buildings, and scenes after the manner of Whistler but also came under the influence of the European artists' revolt from tradition and himself began to produce experimental work. He was especially attracted to the expressionism of Emil Nolde, though much of his work is reminiscent of Goya. Some of the prints of those years reveal wild expression and somber tones and his "strong, scratchy drypoint lines combined with aquatint . . . convey a mood of foreboding gloom. Like the isolated Nolde on the edge of the Baltic Sea, Smith was able to evoke the elemental power of marshes and clouds through new applications of traditional techniques."[47] Smith also experimented with pointillism. The skill he displayed in his more traditional etchings won him a gold medal at the Panama-Pacific International Exposition in San Francisco in 1915. By this time, his etchings were being widely sought by private collectors such as Justice Oliver Wendell Holmes.[48]

Smith's freelance career was interrupted by America's entering World War I. In May, 1917, he began officer's training at Plattsburg, New York. Commissioned a first lieutenant on September 25, 1917, in the Engineer Section of the Officers Reserve Corps, he served for some months in Company B, 40th Engineers. A camouflage unit stationed at Camp American University, Washington, D.C., the 40th was commanded by Homer Saint-Gaudens, son of the well-known artist Augustus Saint-Gaudens.[49]

Smith did not long remain with his camouflage unit. Selected as one of the eight official artists, he was promoted to captain on February 13, 1918, placing him on the same footing with the other artists who entered the army at that rank. However, since he was the only one of the eight to receive formal military training and had been in the service longer, Smith was the senior officer of the group and he was so regarded by the army high command. He was the first of the eight artists to arrive in France, reporting for duty on March 15, 1918.[50]

Capt. Townsend

Harry Everett Townsend was born to William Jarman and Jane Elizabeth (Houghtaling) Townsend in Wyoming, Illinois, on March 10, 1879.[51] His father was a prosperous farmer and merchant. He also operated a peddling wagon, and Harry, as a youth, used it to deliver supplies to farms throughout the countryside. However, he developed an interest in art and soon began to make money by painting signs in the area. Resolving not to follow in his father's business, he took his savings and, on a new bicycle, went to Chicago to enroll in the Art Institute. He worked his way through the school by setting up and servicing farm implements for the McCormick Harvester Company on farms in Illinois and Iowa during the summers. He also made trips to the American Southwest, where he made paintings and sketches of Indians and scenic attractions, to be used in advertisements for the Rock Island and Santa Fe railroads. Among Townsend's teachers at the Art Institute were painters Frederick Freer and Frank Duveneck and sculptor Lorado Taft.

Following the completion of his art studies at Chicago, in 1900 Townsend continued his training under Howard Pyle. He also studied for a time in Europe, in Paris at the Académie Moderne, the Atelier Julien, and Colarossi's studio and worked briefly in London.

Townsend then returned to Chicago to teach in the Academy of Fine Arts. He also married Cory Schiedewend, who had been a fellow student at the Art Institute, on July 20, 1904.

Thereafter, the Townsends departed Chicago for the New York art scene, establishing a home and studio nearby in Leonia, New Jersey. Harry soon rose to the front ranks among illustrators in America, and his work appeared frequently in such major magazines as *Harper's, Century, Everybody's, Scribner's,* and *McClure's,* and as illustrations for books. Townsend also exhibited regularly. He still found time to study sculpture with Herman MacNeil and to further develop his skills in etching, woodcutting, and lithography, acquiring expertise in all forms of pictorial art, from magazine illustration to mural decoration.[52]

In 1912, the Townsends, now with a young daughter, went to Europe, where Harry worked for London magazines. They took up residence in Montreuil-sur-Mer, in northern France, which gave them easy access to both London and Paris. They were in France when the war came in 1914, and they immediately returned to New York, establishing themselves in Greenwich Village, where Harry resumed work for the magazines and book publishers.

When the United States entered the war and began to utilize artists in various ways, Townsend began to draw war posters. While engaged in that activity, Townsend was recommended for the captaincy that would send him to France. Commissioned on March 21, 1918, he reported for duty in Europe on May 1.[53]

3. The Daily Travail

Although the earlier careers of the artists reflected diversity, they were soon to have common experiences in abundance. One was the pleasure and excitement of being commissioned and given an opportunity to serve their country in a way compatible with their skills. Peixotto recalled that when offered his captaincy in February of 1918, he "gladly accepted." Similarly, Tulla Dunn long remembered the night in Leonia when her husband Harvey received a telephone call from the War Department. Asking how long it would take him to get ready to leave for France, he shouted, "Two hours!" That settled, he and his wife took a long drive and discussed what had transpired and what it might mean for their future. "It was a dramatic night," Tulla recalled, "made unusually eerie and unreal by a dazzling display of the *aurora borealis* in the northern sky."[1]

Almost immediately after receiving their commissions, the new captains were ordered to France. Only ten days after receiving his bars Peixotto was on board the *Pocahontas,* an army transport. Formerly the *Princess Irene* of the North German Lloyd fleet, the ship was one of the German vessels commandeered by the American government following its declaration of war. Departing Hoboken "on a rainy, lowery day in March," Peixotto soon found himself discharging official duties such as officer of the day, for which he was ill prepared. In one abandon-ship drill, he was on duty with a lieutenant perhaps as lost as he. "The army is made of strange birds," Peixotto decided, his companion being an ornithologist who had collected rare bird specimens in East Africa for the Smithsonian Institution.[2] Similarly, Harding drew the assignment as officer of the day and was given about five minutes' briefing on his duties—all of the military training he had received to that time. He rather ruefully remarked on the situation: "Twelve days ago I was still a civilian —some difference out here."[3]

Having received his orders in a "state of maximum exuberance," Dunn too experienced the haste with which the War Department proceeded. In short order, he "received his shots, his scanty orientation, and a company of enlisted men to look after during the Atlantic crossing."[4]

But if uncomfortable in their unfamiliar uniforms and no doubt vexing assignments, the trip over hardly lacked interest. To Peixotto's artist eye, the ships that he observed, "brilliantly camouflaged like wasps, queerly striped with black and white, with spots between of yellow, grey-blue, and water-green," or painted with low-visibility colors and "toned like Monet's pictures with spots of pink and green," never failed to fascinate.[5] Other observations made by Peixotto in his book, *The American Front*, were those no doubt common to all of the men. Landing at Saint-Nazaire, he found himself in short order at Engineer Headquarters located at the Caserne des Jardins in Angers. Thence he traveled to General Headquarters, AEF, at Chaumont, in southeastern France on the upper reaches of the Marne River. Only seventeen days had elapsed between the sailing from Hoboken and his arrival there. With an eye for the country and a lively interest in his surroundings, as befits an artist, Peixotto did not fail to record the details of Chaumont, the former French military barracks complex that had been taken over by the American high command.[6]

Despite Chaumont's anticipating their coming, the artists' arrival posed assignment problems, since "an official artist was a strange bird to classify in the army." According to an anecdote circulated after the war by one of Dunn's friends, Dunn's service in France began with a somewhat humorous twist. When he embarked for the front, a bureaucratic tangle placed him in command of a company of infantry. This was a most puzzling situation for the artist who did not even know how to bring his men to attention. After explaining the situation to the troops, who were remarkably understanding of the circumstances, the only thing that seemed appropriate was for Dunn to go on sick call until he could be relieved of his "command" and receive orders for his proper assignment.[7]

After some deliberations it was decided to attach the artists to G-2D, the Press and Censorship Division of the Intelligence Branch (G-2) of the General Staff, AEF. It also seemed logical, after some preliminary searches for other arrangements, to station the eight men at Neufchâteau, a town north of Chaumont, near the front, where the war correspondents accredited to the AEF were also located.[8] Neufchâteau was, in addition, the headquarters of the First Army Corps. Later the U.S. First Army was organized there, and at war's end the town was the Advanced Headquarters of the Services of Supply (SOS). Since the town was the center of so much official activity, Peixotto remembered it as "always crowded with officers, who gathered toward evening in the Club Lafayette for dinner and a smoke afterward in the café."[9]

The artists themselves were consulted as to how they could best accomplish their work. Specific orders resulted, and Captains Morgan, Peixotto, Smith, and Townsend were the first to be instructed in their duties, in a memorandum dated April 30, 1918.[10] They were to "keep in mind the need of supplying sketches and paintings both for historical purposes and for current use in American publications to which these sketches will be distributed thru the War Department." Each artist was to decide for himself which of his works should be retained for future treatment of a more permanent nature, and which should be forwarded for immediate release by Washington. Artists were to submit their monthly output to G-2D, at Headquarters, AEF. Each picture was to bear the title, the name of the artist, where it was made, the date of its composition, and a brief description of the subject. At Headquarters, the art was often used to stage a monthly show for the benefit of Headquarters personnel. From there, the pictures were sent by G-2D to the officer-in-charge, photo sub-section, G-2D, in Paris. He had them censored by the photographic censor, G-2D, and dispatched to the Signal Corps photographic laboratory, also in Paris. There, the works were photographed. Copies were sent to the artists, to the G-2D files at AEF Headquarters, and to the chief of the Military Intelligence Branch at the War Department. The originals were next sent to the Chief, Historical Branch, War Plans Division (formerly the War College Division), General Staff, Washington, D.C. The Historical Branch, only organized in March of 1918, was charged with compiling the pictorial and written record of the war and was the logical agency to take charge of the finished art. Following its arrival in Washington, the art was placed at the disposal of the Committee on Public Information, which was organized to disseminate such works for propaganda purposes. In addition to submitting their artwork at Headquarters, each artist was instructed to prepare a monthly report briefly describing his work for the preceding thirty days, the tasks pending, and those planned for the coming month.

Later, on June 7, 1918, G-2D prepared another memorandum, entitled "General Policy Reference the Work of Official Artists," which included additional details.[11] This document stipulated that as long as the field was covered, the artists were allowed "considerable latitude" in doing their work. They were issued a permanent pass, signed by both the American and French high commands, giving them substantial freedom in their movements. They used it to full advantage. However, it was also the army's intention to keep in close touch with the artists, "in order that [it] may derive greatest benefit from the talent of these officers and for the reason that any inefficient member may be known." Therefore, the men also traveled under written instructions so that their location might be known at all times to their superiors. Nevertheless, these directions were drafted in such a way that the artists' work schedules were as elastic as possible, enabling them to take advantage of the greatest opportunities for productive work.

Three areas of operations would constitute their working sites: troops in the trenches, troops in training bases and in reserve, and the lines of communication. In general, the men divided themselves into two rather distinct groups: those who were chiefly interested in drawing the figure and those whose interest and training was more along the lines of landscape and architectural work. The former group was composed of Morgan, Dunn, Harding, and Aylward; the latter, of Peixotto, Duncan, and Smith, with Townsend covering some of both. The first group accordingly devoted more of its attention to drawing the men in billets and trenches and the general movement of troops, while the second recorded the activities of the AEF in general, from the ports of debarkation, through the Services of Supply, and to and including the fighting front. To be sure, as time elapsed, there was considerable blurring of the lines between the two groups, and their pictures do not fall easily into the two categories.

The artists naturally had to spend some time in more or less informal training and orientation. As Smith once described it to Colonel Steese back in Washington: "We found ourselves going through a process of schooling which, I think, came to us all as a surprise. I don't think it occurred to any of us that like our brother officers in the various branches of the Army we too would have to pass through a period of training. But it has been exactly that and it is only recently that there has grown up a feeling of confidence in our group in regard to our work and our ability to handle it in the way we feel that it should be handled."[12] It took some time, then, for the artists to become accustomed to military ways. Also, the details of equipment, such as artillery, motor trucks, wagons, and aircraft, as well as all other matériel of a modern army, had to be mentally digested before pictures could be reproduced with accuracy. All of this caused some delay in the artists' production of acceptable work. In addition, considerable time was taken up in locating and purchasing materials, in settling into their billets, and finding studios in which to work.[13]

Other factors had bearing on their art, as Smith explained to Steese. He and his colleagues were surprised and perhaps a little disappointed to find that the war was not altogether as expected. They, like most people at home, had been fed on highly charged war books which contained exaggerated war pictures. They were therefore expecting to find the whole of France "a seething battlefield." Instead, there were large areas of calm, and even at the front, the artists, expecting to find thrilling "'over-the-top' material," often only recorded impressions of a quiet night in a dugout. Of course, things would change as the Americans became increasingly committed to action, but for some time Smith could only conclude that "our drawings will be open to the charge of being unwarlike and reflecting conditions of life over [here] that seem too peaceful and calm." His answer in advance to such critics was that the artists endeavored to portray military life as truthfully and honestly as possible, "without resorting to sensational tricks and fakes."[14]

Equipped with two National automobiles, the artists proceeded from their base at Neufchâteau to visit the various sectors in which Americans were beginning to operate.[15] Thereafter, an artist making sketches near the scenes of action became a familiar, if sometimes misunderstood, sight.

The men naturally developed their own agendas and individual styles of operation and conduct. A close examination of how some of them worked will illustrate their methods and what they accomplished. Morgan, for instance, carried small sketchbooks, measuring about five by six inches, in which he made hurried notes with his pencil. Most of these sketches were little more than shorthand scribbles, as unintelligible to the non-artist as stenographic notes. To Morgan, though, they were valuable aids to the memory, being records of his impressions. These rough sketches became the basis of finished drawings which he produced in his studio. Later, when making his illustrations, Morgan, following the technique that he had long since developed, assumed that his first drawing would be his final one. Never using preliminary sketches, if his original sketch did not suit him, he simply discarded it and made a fresh start. His favorite medium was charcoal, though he used ink, wash, and color. He preferred a brush to a pen when making line drawings.[16]

As was the case with most of the artists, Morgan did his initial sketching near Neufchâteau, specifically at such locations as Baccarat, Sanzey, and Andilly, in the Toul Sector, where American troops were engaged in intense training.

Morgan, who often traveled with Duncan, then ranged farther afield. He especially favored the 2d Division, notably its Marine brigade, and followed it into action at Château-Thierry and Belleau Wood.[17] As late summer arrived, with the sustained Allied advance well under way, Morgan followed the troops into the St. Mihiel salient and on into the Argonne Forest, attempting to capture in his art what the fighting on those battlefields was like, seeking to make a permanent record while the scenes of combat were still fresh in his mind.[18]

Morgan also found time to do some illustrating for the *Stars and Stripes*. In July, he accompanied Townsend to Paris to make sketches of American troops on parade in the French capital as part of the Bastille Day celebrations.[19]

Townsend early developed an interest in the technology of the war, making it his specialty. He was fascinated, for instance, by the large 240-mm naval guns, mounted on railcars, that were operating with the 26th Division. Likewise exhibiting an interest in tanks, he visited the light tank center at Bourg, near Langres, in August, making several pictures.[20] He also executed several studies of planes in the First Aero Pursuit Group of the U.S. Army's Air Service. His interest in aircraft stemmed in part from his brother's having served, before his untimely death, with a British Royal Flying Corps squadron. Maturing as an artist of aerial scenes, Townsend painted some of his more memorable aircraft pictures in September as he followed the airmen into action. As soon as was practicable after the Armistice, Townsend made detailed studies of captured German aircraft. He took at least one flight with an American pilot, so as to more closely observe air operations, although he did not experience actual combat during the flight.[21]

Not all of the significant activity of the AEF occurred at the front, however. The support of the men in the lines required a huge supply system which needed to be recorded as well. Duncan was one of the artists who spent considerable time with the Services of Supply. Much of July, 1918, he spent at Angers, site of a heavy artillery school and ordnance and salvage shops, and at the port of Brest, the principal American embarkation and debarkation center. At these locations, Duncan depicted the mundane but vital activities carried on far to the rear.[22]

One of the most active of the artists was Peixotto, probably because of his familiarity with the French scene. He was plainly very much at home, often serving as interpreter and guide for his less culturally acclimated colleagues. Nevertheless, the military realities dictated how much of his effort would be expended. He too had to go where the troops were, accommodating himself to the conditions of war. On April 20, together with Smith and Morgan, Peixotto was at Baccarat, spending a week in the area of the 42d or "Rainbow" Division, composed of National Guard units from many different states, hence its name. From there, the artists proceeded to Lorraine, where other U.S. troops were billeted in various villages.[23]

During May, Peixotto made three separate trips to various areas. On the ninth, he was with the 2d Division near Verdun. There he visited the Marine brigade of this division, spending one evening with a company commander, in order to soak up atmosphere. On May 14, he joined the 26th Division, a National Guard division from New England, at Boucq, and on May 23, he was with the 32d Division in Alsace.[24]

Peixotto was even busier in June, going to Paris for supplies; Dijon and its motor transport shops and camouflage plant; Is-sur-Tille, where there were ordnance shops and the largest bakery in the AEF; and Langres, the location of the Army General Staff school and a large hospital. He then made two trips to the Toul Sector, and late in the month, went to the Châteatu-Thierry front. He was under fire for much of this visit and later experienced a night air raid at Le Ferté-sous-Jouarre, which made a distinct impression on him.[25]

The Toul Sector was of special interest because Domrémy, the birthplace of Joan of Arc, was located there. Since the great heroine's house was only six miles north of Neufchâteau, it was a favorite place to visit for the large numbers of American soldiers present in the vicinity. As Peixotto noted, "I have seen (and I confess that a lump arose in my throat as I saw it) French regiments march by it at salute —the officers raising their swords to their chins, then sweeping them outward at arm's length; the men turning their eyes fixedly upon the sacred spot."[26]

The months of June, July, and August found Peixotto and Smith, who often worked together, at such bases as Nevers, an important railroad and storage center; Tours, headquarters of the SOS and an aviation instruction center; Saint-Nazaire, the principal AEF freight port; and Bourges, with its railroad and ordnance shops. Taking time to visit the Château-Thierry Sector repeatedly, on July 4, Peixotto was in Paris making drawings of the Independence Day gala which the French staged for their American allies.[27]

The pace quickened in September, though early in the month Peixotto's experiences were serene enough. He completed trips to Nevers and Issoudun, where many of the great air bases of the U.S. Army Air Service were located.[28] But Peixotto recalls dining on September 10 at the Lafayette Club in Neufchâteau with a friend of his, Frank Sibley, correspondent on one of the Boston newspapers and accredited to the New England 26th Division. Sibley strongly suggested that something was "in the air," being certain that the nipping off of the "hernia of St. Mihiel" was being planned. Eagerly, Peixotto and Morgan accompanied Sibley back to his division. They arrived in time for the St. Mihiel action, and Peixotto closely followed the troops' progress. He was especially gratified at seeing the commander of the French armies, Gen. Henri Pétain, and Gen. John J. Pershing enter St. Mihiel on September 13, "a date forever memorable in American history." The U.S. Secretary of War, Newton D. Baker, and the French premier, Georges Clemenceau, also soon arrived in the captured city.[29] Meanwhile, Peixotto busily recorded scenes in such places as Seicheprey, Rambucourt, Apremont, and Bouillonville.[30]

The great Allied push that began on September 26, 1918, found Peixotto with the American forces at Clermont-en-Argonne, awaiting the expected assault, and in October he made two trips to the Argonne forest, which had seen such bitter fighting. After following the men for several days, Peixotto took up a temporary headquarters at Rarecourt, in a deserted room with a "fireless fireplace and leaky ceiling." From this refuge, he made various sketching trips, the conditions of which he once graphically described: "Rain and slush; mud and dirt; my paper wet and soggy, my hands numb with cold—these were the conditions, none too propitious for sketching, that obtained in the Argonne in October."[31] This exposure no doubt contributed to Peixotto's becoming ill late in October. He was summarily ordered by Maj. A. L. James, Jr., then chief, G-2D, to retire for two weeks to his studio home, which he still maintained at Samois-sur-Seine, to recuperate and to finish such works as his health permitted. He quickly availed himself of this opportunity.[32]

Peixotto went to Paris during his convalescence, there witnessing the coming of the Armistice. Arriving on Sunday, November 10, he noted that the populace was already anticipating what was to come. The boulevards were packed, and people strolled about the Place de la Concorde, which was lined with captured German aircraft such as the infamous *Fokkers*, *Rumplers*, and *Gothas*. Guns were there in great numbers, flanked by *Minenwerfers* and trench mortars. A German tank had been placed at the entrance to the Tuileries, and there also "the statues of Lille and Strasbourg, so long in mourning, were now gayly decorated with flags and wreaths."[33]

On the memorable day, Peixotto went to the Paris offices of G-2D, at Rue Ste. Anne. There he was informed that the Armistice had been signed early that morning and was to take effect at eleven. As he looked at his watch, "it stood at eleven-ten. The war was over!" From a balcony of a big office building that fronts on the Place de l'Opéra, Peixotto observed the great celebrations that occurred later in the day and evening.[34]

Though busier than most of the artists, Peixotto's activities were typical. However, his frequent traveling companion Smith, as officer-in-charge of the artists, had his own duties and agendas. As the first of the men to arrive in France, Smith took advantage of his initial stay at Headquarters to make several sketches of the buildings and the town. These included Pershing's residence. The most prolific of the artists by far, Smith had in a few days done eight pictures, which he transmitted to G-2D in early May, the first official art to be completed.[35]

One of Smith's duties was to arrange the monthly exhibits of the official AEF art at Headquarters at Chaumont. Under the auspices of the Historical Section, GHQ, these shows became a regular affair and gave officers of the high command opportunity to view the art being painted in France before it was shipped to Washington.[36]

Harding, unlike the other artists, used a camera to assist him in gathering on-the-scene material. But like the others, his first work was done in the area near Neufchâteau, especially the Toul Sector. In June, he ranged farther afield, joining the troops at Château-Thierry.[37]

July was a busy month for Harding, and he spent several days with the 3d Division troops in their advance lines, accompanying them when they began to cross the Marne, proceeding from Mont St. Père to La Charmel and Jaulgonne. Harding was exhilarated: "I was in the latter place [Jaulgonne] when [the] enemy was on [an] overlooking hill. The material gathered was to my mind wonderful." Harding once explained to the chief, G-2D, how he functioned: "At the front I make as many as sixty sketches or notes during a trip, besides constant observations," he noted. Conditions at the front made it impossible for him to complete the sketches as finished works, and he saw his trips into combat areas as the opportunity to gather material, usually much more than he needed, which would later be turned into completed pictures at his leisure.[38]

Unquestionably, Harding's long training in careful study of occurrences and scenes around him aided his wartime artistic endeavors. His diary reveals his keenness and awareness as to how impressions might be transferred to canvas:

> Pass French motor trucks on road, they raise clouds of dust that cover the leeward side, trees and fields like a white frost. We ran to one side for miles through woods over ridges. Pass a platoon of French cavalry with a hundred Boche prisoners just captured over near Belleau. They are stolid types, some like professors with glasses, or short and stocky, all with coats off, shirts open, hands swinging and all covered white like the fields.

Another entry graphically described an otherwise commonplace scene:

> Down the road comes a French Division General and two of his staff. He walks as if in Paris in peacetime—cane in hand, helmet on, gas mask hanging. He vaults a low hedge, picks a rosebud and puts it in his lapel buttonhole, picks two more roses, and vaults the hedge again; gives one to each of his aides. He does not see us fifty feet away walking behind a hedge. Maybe after three years training I can do it too. Four shells fall in quick succession, then four more bracketing the road. The French General still sticks to the road.

Harding did not overlook a blown-up bridge, with its "two maimed piers from which the arch springs—a gaping wound in the centre—like two shoulders each with the upper arm shot off." He further described "the intimate state of undress of a house just hit by a shell. Rooms open up intimately—beds unmade—dishes still on [the] dining-room table, pots still on the stove, curtains blowing gently through the dust and smoke and flame." Such keen powers of observation were bound to result in art of some interest, if the artist possessed the requisite skill, as Harding surely did.[39]

Nevertheless, Harding's attention to detail resulted in drawings in which he was more concerned with the effect of the war on the persons involved rather than on scenes depicted with photographic precision or on panoramic sweeps of the battlefields, all in his own impressionistic style.

One of the more thoughtful of the eight artists, Harding later reflected upon the difficulties of creating good war art under the adverse circumstances. Even with the usual difficulties of transport—the two autos were never adequate—and other problems to overcome, "there still confronts the artist the problems of his craft, to be solved perhaps in a cold drenching rain, with a sketch book held under one's trench coat making each pencil mark mean something." The sketch secured, the artist was unable to rush to a studio to record it while the impression was fresh, and he simply tramped on, adding to his notes, not for a day, but perhaps for a week, during which time he was fortunate to average a meal a day and a few hours of sleep.[40]

Then, too, "it is the loneliest place in the world," just behind an enemy artillery barrage, which was hardly conducive to the production of exhibition pictures which critics seemed to expect could be produced at the front. Harding continued: "After a week with the advance one's power of observation dulled, your head, [and] your sketch book were filled with impressions; and weary and footsore one returned to the working billet—in my own case a little French kitchen twelve by sixteen feet." There he was normally able to produce two drawings or so per day. Then, having straightened out the preliminary sketches, the fear of missing something drove the artist back to the fighting line, "each trip always adding material, always learning something by experience, and always plunging in full of enthusiasm, and coming out with a realization of inadequacy, that one was not artist enough to get it [all down properly]." However, undoubtedly at least some of the artists succeeded. Harding was of the opinion that the work of Morgan and Dunn in particular had succeeded in capturing "a certain spirit of the war," and he attempted to do so as well. Major Banning, for one, was certain that Harding had succeeded; indeed, he was convinced that Harding had produced the best of all the art created by the American official artists.[41]

Nevertheless, Harding was not entirely satisfied with his work, being aware that "the man who produces anything out of this war has more than new technical problems to solve, he has much new material to master, and with the best traditions of the past, produce an art of his own epoch." Most certainly, he concluded, those who had been to France must attempt to produce a great war art, and were they to succeed, they would "unquestionably be assured a position in the front rank of contemporary art."[42] He later attempted to accomplish this himself. After taking six months following his discharge "to put [my] field notes in some sort of shape before it was too late," in 1920 he produced his portfolio, *The American Expeditionary Forces in Action*. It consisted of thirty-eight color plates, and five hundred copies of the book were privately printed and sold. If not the great war art he aspired to, the collection is a notable one and makes a contribution to an understanding of the American experience in World War I.[43]

Long before that publishing event, in August of 1918, Harding was in the Vesle area. Becoming especially interested in the German positions captured there, he made numerous careful drawings of them and spent considerable time interviewing the American troops engaged in combat operations in the area. September found him with the advance troops, accompanying the first detachments to push off from Beaumont, through to Pannes, Beney, and St. Benoît, as they worked along the line to Hattonchâtel during the St. Mihiel campaign. Harding also witnessed the hard fighting at Varennes and Montfaucon later in the month, when the Americans launched the Meuse-Argonne offensive.[44]

October was spent in the Argonne Forest. There Harding devoted considerable time to making notes on how the troops lived in the open, a new phase of American campaigning in France.[45] The Armistice found him at Sedan on the Meuse River, in a good position to follow the forward movements of the Army of Occupation from Pont-à-Mousson to Metz and Briey, through to Luxembourg and the German border.

Harvey Dunn, as his biographer has observed, "went to Europe with a fervent desire to picture the war as it really was—'the shock and loss and bitterness and blood of it.'" And he plunged into his work with zeal and energy. In addition to his imposing physical size, Dunn was conspicuous in that he carried a large portable sketch box designed with two rollers upon which was rolled his sketching paper. When a drawing was finished, Dunn merely wound the sketch around one roller, exposing a new sketching surface in the process.[46]

In addition to his unique sketch box, Dunn equipped himself with a Hohner "Marine Band" harmonica, key of C, which he carried with him on his sketching excursions, this too enhancing his presence among the troops. Thus, "Dunn's bigness, his sense of the dramatic, his dominant and sometimes bluff manner was clearly evident in his actions on the battlefield."[47]

Dunn's work was rather unusual, though as he once explained: "The pictures which I am delivering are of no specific place or organization and while, consequently, may be lacking in fact, are not, however, barren of truth in so far as I have succeeded in expressing in them the character of the struggle and the men engaged." Furthermore, though Dunn made numerous sketches, he completed less than thirty pictures while in the AEF, well below the average of the group, which collectively produced more than five hundred works. He argued that neither the facilities available nor the time at his disposal allowed him to carry out "in a more permanent medium certain work of an important nature that I have in mind and which eventually must be done." The rapid progress and great activity on the front precluded any pauses for careful drawing and painting.[48] Yet, in oils, watercolors, pastels, crayon, and charcoal, Dunn created some art of high quality, and as art expert Edgar M. Howell has suggested, in later years these works had emerged as by far the most popular of all the AEF combat art, possessing "an undeniable appeal which most of the pictures of his fellow artists oddly lack." Howell felt that this popularity was the result of the successful "projection of [Dunn's] self-image, his ideal of the 'universal man at war,' and his forceful representation of this point of view." His art also possessed a "stark, brutal . . . quality that has drawn people to his work. This was war as they imagined it. This was the war they wanted to see." Dunn came to see that "war was a series of individual struggles of individual men, in a sea of masses and machines." These men, as Dunn painted them, "knew exultation, fear and fatigue. They knew the triumph, the frustration and anonymity of combat."[49]

In producing this work, Dunn followed the well-trodden path. He, too, was familiar with the Toul Sector, Château-Thierry, and St. Mihiel, where in September he attached himself to Company A, 1st Battalion, 167th Infantry, staying with them in action until they reached their objective. Once more, Dunn found that because of the bad weather and the extremely rapid advance, he was unable to make sketches, though the mental impressions that he formed were of more value in any case. When he got the opportunity, he would "render these impressions in pictorial form." He was later along the front from Neuville to Montfaucon, in the Meuse-Argonne, where he was also hurried, though in the course of the month managed to complete six pictures.[50]

In October, Dunn painted four more pictures and also spent several days on the front north of Verdun collecting material and impressions for others. November was another hectic month, with the war rushed to a conclusion, and once more Dunn reported that he had no opportunity to complete any work because of the rapid pace of events. He hoped that there was no hurry now that the Armistice had been signed and the need for propaganda pictures was gone. In the new circumstances "it seemed best that I further familiarize myself with war conditions which at once . . . began rapidly to disappear from our various fronts, and to become acquainted with the environs of our armies of occupation." He would also soon need a suitable studio enabling him to produce—as he always insisted upon —work of "a more permanent character than that which I have yet done."[51]

The myriad activities and accomplishments of the artists were not without controversy, however. Though the artists were guided by the instructions which they themselves had had a hand in preparing, there remained differences of opinion as to what they were to accomplish. Also, questions regarding both quantity and quality of the art arose soon after the artists' arrival in Europe. It was not long before criticism of the artists' work began to arrive in France from Washington. In July, 1918, the chief of staff, Gen. Peyton C. March, sent a cable to Pershing stating the "amount of work received here indicates unsatisfactory results from this personnel. Very desirable to have such work done well. Your comment desired."[52] Pershing replied that the work of the official artists seemd "fairly satisfactory." He described the tribulations under which the artists worked and the great difficulty in obtaining materials. He was disposed to give the artists a "reasonable time in which to demonstrate their worth," also being aware that their work was of a nature making it difficult to judge its value as promptly "as would be possible in [a] purely military endeavor." The work then in transit to Washington would show "that they are doing reasonably well," Pershing continued, noting that some of the art that was by then appearing at GHQ "has received hearty approval of critics." He therefore recommended that the artists continue as they had been, "until it is clearly apparent that their work is unsatisfactory."[53]

However, criticism continued in Washington. Major Banning, by then chief of the Pictorial Section of the Historical Branch, War Plans Division, General Staff in Washington, and who had a hand in the launching of the official artist program, was one of the most vocal of the critics. Writing Capt. J. André Smith in mid-August of 1918, he asserted that, regarding the early examples of the combat art to arrive in Washington, "neither the magazine editors for whom the pictures are largely intended, nor the officers of the General Staff appear to express very much interest in [them]," he began. The pictures did not seem to serve either a military or a propaganda purpose. The work of the AEF's artists was often unfavorably compared with the splendid color reproductions, especially the work of François Flameng, in the French Magazine *L'Illustration*. His pictures showing all aspects of the war were "splendidly alive, and real" and dealt with subjects that could not be handled by photography. Banning pointedly insisted that "it is pictures of this kind that we expect from you official artists." Indeed, "practically all of the official pictures received from the official artists of the A.E.F. to date, have the gentle and quiet atmosphere of the city studio. They lack action and they lack human interest," he complained. Further, they treated topics that had "been treated hundreds and thousands of times with the camera." He was further disturbed that no pictures had as yet been received from Aylward, Harding, Townsend, or Dunn, and he asked, "What has become of these men? What disposition is made of their drawings?"[54]

Elsewhere in the War Department, others were similarly dissatisfied, as is demonstrated in the official reply to Pershing's cable in late August. This generally concurred with Banning's criticisms and ordered the artists assigned to duty where civilians did not have access and that they produce action pictures, particularly drawings made in the zone of the advance.[55]

Pershing replied that by mid-September of 1918 some 283 pictures had been turned in at GHQ, including works by all of the artists. As to the continuing criticism, Pershing could only reiterate that the Historical Sub-Section of the General

Staff at his headquarters expressed "heartiest approval of these artists' work." The Sub-Section was also of the opinion "that a highly important function of their work is to preserve these scenes in the zone of operations and elsewhere for the historical record of the war as well as to provide current needs in periodicals." Pershing also reminded Washington that regarding action pictures, "It is out of the question to have any artist at work in front line trenches or anywhere near them during active engagement," though some of the artists persisted in working close to the action.[56] However, the general did recognize the validity of some of the complaints and ordered that the War Department's instructions regarding confining the artists to the advance zone be obeyed. The artists were also instructed to make "a special effort to portray action wherever possible."[57]

In response to the criticism from Washington, Maj. A. L. James, Jr., then chief of G-2D, on October 20, 1918, instructed Captain Smith to draft a full report on the official artists, how they came to be appointed, how they conceived of their duties, and other relevant matters. Seeing an opportunity to set the record straight and to present the artists' views, Smith complied, submitting a lengthy document to which he attached a copy of a column from the *New York Times*, February 22, 1918, describing the selection and commissioning of the artists and the exchanges of letters between Major Banning and himself.

In the first place, there was a basic misunderstanding, Smith asserted, as to what sort of pictures were required and how they were to be used. Major Banning and others in Washington plainly wanted a large quantity of work for use in current publications. This was "entirely opposed" to the use of the French and British war art, which the AEF painters used as a model. Smith was certain that this was the major point of contention. "I am very sure," he continued, "that we all accepted our commissions with the firm belief that we would primarily serve the Government as artists chosen along the line of our particular and individual field of work and with the idea that the sum-total of our drawings, paintings, and etchings would form a separate and distinct pictorial record of the war, valuable not only as historical documents but also as works of art." To be sure, the artists did recognize that many of their works would be suitable for current publication. However, "That we would be required to enter upon a basis of a regular monthly shipment of drawings for use in magazines for propaganda and sensational illustrations had never occurred to us nor was such a possibility at any time suggested to us," Smith protested. This demand had resulted in a hurried manner of working which could only be detrimental to the quality of the art produced. The opportunity for a more leisurely contemplation and study, and the gathering of material for future use, "which is a necessary part of our work, has been lost to us." Also, the limitation of their field of operation to the advance zone, as Pershing had ordered, was "a clear defeat of the true object for which we have been sent here," which was to record activities throughout the AEF.

General Black had been quoted in the *New York Times* article referred to as saying that the artists were mainly expected to make "a pictorial record of the war." Smith and the others had also been informed that Washington would forward specific instructions to France. But none had been forthcoming. He and some of the others had to help draw up a report on the nature and purpose of the work, and they had had to find their own studios and materials. After Lt. Col. Walter C. Sweeney, chief, G-2D, received a request from Washington for an immediate shipment of drawings, Smith, Morgan, and Peixotto made a hurried trip to the front and hastily executed seventeen drawings. These were sent to Washington, which responded with the demand that a regular monthly shipment of pictures be made. In this way, the "insidious formula" was established, based on either a change of policy in Washington, or a misunderstanding always harbored there regarding "the exact nature of our work and our method of working." This "formula" failed to take into account individual differences in method "as well as our particular lines of work." While it was true that Sweeney's general instructions made it clear that the selection and number of drawings were best determined by the individual artist, Smith felt that "nevertheless, . . . the desire to be represented each month as fully as possible . . . acted against our own desires in the matter and brought about the feeling of pressure and haste."[58] Moreover, the monthly exhibitions held at Chaumont, soon a regular feature, were an added burden to the monthly shipment plan. They did, it is true, serve a useful purpose in that officers who were familiar with the life and surroundings that the artists were recording were generally favorable to what was produced. This helped to counter the nettlesome complaints from Washington.

To their credit, the artists' superiors in France defended them. Maj. Robert M. Johnston, head of the Historical Sub-Section, GHQ, AEF, wrote to Col. C. W. Weeks, chief of the Historical Branch in Washington and Banning's superior, making it clear he was well satisfied with the artwork being produced. He further noted that the officers at GHQ agreed with the artists that the works should mainly serve as historical records, while still being used for propaganda purposes. The officers at Chaumont were also of the opinion that only personnel in France could properly assess the pictures as to their merits as military art. Maj. A. L. James, Jr., chief of G-2D, concurred, praising the artists for performing their duties in an exemplary manner. He expressed the view that it was not fair for Banning to criticize the work of the artists "inasmuch as the artists are prohibited by military protocol from answering him direct in their own defense." He strongly suggested that Banning be prohibited from writing the artists personally, having recourse only to military channels. This was apparently done.[59]

Before any ban on writing directly to the artists went into effect, Banning again wrote to Captain Smith. This letter, dated September 30, 1918, had an entirely different tone. By then much better art had arrived in Washington, and Banning was very encouraged. Several high-ranking officers were also pleased with the quality of the newly arrived pictures. The work of Harding had received special commendation from many of those who had seen it.[60]

By the end of the year, the art was being generally well received in America. Some was displayed at the Corcoran Art Gallery in Washington under the supervision of the Committee on Public Information and the American Federation of Arts. The exhibition then proceeded to New York City as part of the Allied War Salon. From there the show went to Pittsburgh and other cities. While the art was in New York, the editors of the principal magazines met to select some of the art for publication. Some forty of the drawings were chosen, ranging from *Everybody's Magazine's* twelve, to the single selection made by *Literary Digest*.[61]

The artists in France therefore found themselves emerging from under the cloud of disapproval. One of the results of the change in the attitude in Washington was that the artists continued to be given as much latitude as possible, and "very wisely no attempt was made to direct their work along exact lines."[62]

The artists were finally being better received at home, but this had generally been the case in France all along. They were also usually extended the full cooperation of commanders in the field. Occasionally, when some commander was especially helpful, a warm letter from the chief, G-2D, was forthcoming. Such a letter was sent to Col. Ulysses G. McAlexander, of the 38th U.S. Infantry, in August, 1918, by Lt. Col. E. R. W. McCabe. It mentioned how pleased Smith and Peixotto had been at their reception by that outfit, emphasizing the courtesy and kindness accorded them.[63]

However, there was at least one glaring exception. Early in the artists' career, Peixotto found himself confronted by a Lieutenant Colonel Waldo, of the 126th Infantry, then at Soppe-le-Bas. As Peixotto reported, on May 25, 1918, while he was engaged in the performance of his duty and standing on the steps of the Headquarters of the 126th Infantry Regiment, he was addressed by Waldo. "He strongly criticized the policy of having captains attached to the A.E.F. as official artists," Peixotto began. When the artist tried to convince him of the uses of his work, Waldo became "offensively insistent on his own point of view," stating artistic work "was no way to win the war." In response to Peixotto's counterargument that France and Great Britain used commissioned official artists, Waldo replied, "that is why they are not winning the war." McCabe, being apprised of the facts, requested a full report with the recommendation that higher authority give the matter attention.[64] By the endorsement route, the incident proceeded from G-2D to the commanding general of the 32d Division, Maj. Gen. William G. Haan, from there down the chain to the 63d Infantry Brigade, commanded by Brig. Gen. Louis C. Covell, who interrogated Waldo. Waldo, no doubt bewildered by this turn of events, gave his side of the story. He admitted the argument, although he said that it was over the relative merits of photography as opposed to artwork. Waldo claimed he was unaware that Peixotto was working in an official capacity, having decided that he was merely making sketches "of his own volition," or that Peixotto had previously reported to General Haan, who had taken "personal pains to assist him in his work." Haan also greatly regretted the incident and formally admonished Colonel Waldo, who asserted that he had not intended to criticize AEF policy.[65] There the matter rested, though Peixotto later sent to General Haan reproductions of some of the paintings he had made in the 32d Division's area.[66] Apparently in all other respects the artists received every courtesy and facility for performing their work in the field.

Nevertheless, the artists could not do everything expected of them. The high command of the AEF was under the impression that the official artists were equipped to take care of every requirement. However, apparently only Townsend knew anything about portraiture and his specialty was oil rather than pastel, which the Historical Section in Washington wanted to use to complete a planned project. After the Armistice, as soon as it was obvious that the division commanders would soon be departing their commands the decision was made to have all of their portraits painted "with the greatest possible expedition."[67] A cable was sent to Washington from France requesting that two additional artists, expert in pastel portraiture work, be sent abroad immediately to undertake the work. For some reason, the Secretary of War disapproved, and only later was such portrait painting placed in the hands of Joseph Cummings Chase.[68]

4. After the Armistice

Following the Armistice, the artists continued to work at their assignments. However, their paths began to diverge almost as rapidly as they had merged.

Aylward   Aylward's endeavors in France during the months before the end of the war were similar to those of the others. After the Armistice, he was with the occupation forces that marched through Luxembourg into Germany. Remaining for only a short time on the Rhine, Aylward, like the other artists, desired to relocate in Paris, and he engaged a studio apartment at No. 5 Schoelcher for three months, beginning on February 1, 1919, to use as his base of operations.[1] Meanwhile, he requested permission to cover, pictorially, the activities at the several ports of debarkation, which would best suit his talents. "I should like to make one oil painting, important in size, representative of each Port, and supplement this by watercolor sketches delineating the chief characteristics of individual harbors with transports disembarking troops, unloading supplies, etc.," he explained. He had earlier presented these ideas to GHQ, which tentatively approved, though their execution had to be postponed "by the importance of the activities on the front," a reference to the instructions that the artists must confine themselves to the combat zone. With the cessation of hostilities, Aylward felt that the time had come to do that sort of work.[2]

Aylward soon received orders to proceed to Marseilles, Bordeaux, Le Havre, and other ports he wanted to visit.[3] He believed that this activity would keep him busy until well into the summer, and he desired to continue working out of his

Paris studio until July 15 or so. He agreed to remain in the army after that date if the War Department so desired.

So Aylward went to Marseilles and Bordeaux, as ordered, visiting and making numerous pictures of the huge Bassens Docks. He also painted scenes at La Rochelle, La Pallice, and Rochefort. Finishing his work ahead of schedule, on May 11, 1919, he sought to be relieved from duty as of June 1.[4] He also had other requests. Remembering the trip over, he asked that he be excused from military duty en route to the United States. His motives were two: he did not feel any better qualified than before to command troops, and he wanted "to avoid possible delay in being detailed, as a casual officer, to take command of a detachment of returning troops."[5] In this way, he was hoping to escape being detained at one of the hated casual camps. Conditions were notoriously bad in most of the camps, and the flu epidemic, a major international problem that eventually caused an estimated 20 million deaths worldwide, was rampant. Many soldiers, having escaped from the violence of war, died of the dreaded disease in these surroundings. However, Aylward's departure directly from Marseilles could not be arranged as he had requested, and he had to leave France from the casual camp at St. Aignan. In any event, he was soon home.[6]

Aylward resumed his career as illustrator and writer and later taught art. From 1930 to 1934, he was on the faculty of the Pennsylvania Institute of Art. In 1936, he joined the staff of the School of Fine and Industrial Arts in Newark, New Jersey, where he remained for over a decade. He also taught at the Pratt Institute in Brooklyn. In 1950, he published an art manual in his specialty: *Ships and How to Draw Them.*

Remaining one of the lesser known of the eight AEF combat artists, Aylward died in 1957. But if not as well known in later years as some of his colleagues, Aylward produced some of the most beautiful of the war art. In it, his love for the sea is evident. While his dock pictures do not seem to conjure up the war experience, hard work in the rear areas occupied many doughboys and remained *their* war. Logistics was, after all, central to the American effort, and the scenes were therefore legitimate subjects for an official artist of the AEF.

After the Armistice Duncan also accompanied the troops into Luxembourg and Germany. He found the Moselle Valley especially congenial to his brush and pencil, and December found him on the Rhine.[7]

It is not certain when Duncan took up residence in Paris, but it was probably

Duncan

in late December. He established himself in the Hôtel de Nice, in the Rue des Beaux-Arts. He spent the first three months of the new year in working up drawings and lithographs from sketches made at the front, the completion of which he was sure in April would occupy him for some time.[8] This consideration prompted him to request permission to remain in France even after G-2 ceased operations there, which it was soon scheduled to do. Brig. Gen. D. E. Nolan, head of intelligence, desiring that "we do not want to get any impression started that we are trying to hurry the official artists through their work" and not wanting to place them under someone else in France, asked the War Department to allow Duncan to remain in France under Washington's direct supervision. However, Washington thought otherwise, and on June 14, 1919, Duncan received his orders to Brest for transportation home.[9]

Duncan was soon a civilian and resumed his work as illustrator. In 1925, he became an instructor in drawing and composition at the Art Students' League in New York City, remaining there for several years. In 1939, Harper's published his book, *First Aid to Pictorial Composition*. Then suddenly, on April 11, 1941, the sixty-year-old bachelor died of a stroke while working in his New York studio. Even less well known than Aylward following the war, Duncan remains the most obscure of the official artists.

Dunn

If Duncan was the most obscure of the official artists, Dunn was to be the best known in the postwar years. And he could hardly wait to get home. Dunn immediately decided that since his work "always consisted of pictures of a dramatic character, and now that 'the war is over' and the scenes where the fighting occurred are rapidly changing in character making the obtaining of material more and more difficult," he thought that he should be ordered home, where he could "carry out certain impressions in pictorial form that have been presented to my mind, the success of which requires normal conditions and harmonious surroundings such as do not exist for me here." Dunn was of the opinion that this work would require from three months to a year or more to complete, and he expressed his willingness to return to France, visiting the battlefields at the corresponding time of year that those actions took place.[10]

Shortly thereafter, Dunn and Harding, who were working together, departed from Brest on board the battleship U.S.S. *North Carolina*. They were the first artists to leave, and the only ones to sail home on a warship. They landed back in the United States on February 9, 1919.[11]

Although many of the official artists desired to prolong their services to the army and some were able to do so at least for a time, Dunn was discharged on April 26, 1919. His disappointment was keen. He had envisioned many months, even years, of painting, maybe at the War College, and of having the leisure to turn his sketches, his visions and impressions of the war, into finished works of art. Such was not to be. His premature—as he saw it—discharge left him with a sense of frustration and of a task left undone. He did visit the old battlefields with his son in 1925, but his feelings of rejection remained acute. He was partially able to redress the balance when, in January of 1928, he began to paint covers for the *American Legion Monthly*, many based on his wartime sketches.[12]

In the meantime, Dunn moved his family to Tenafly, New Jersey, a few miles north of Leonia, which was to be his home until his death in 1952. Near his house he built a large studio, which also became a teaching locale. When classes began to overflow that space, he accepted an offer to join the faculty of the Grand Central School of Art in New York City in 1926. In the years thereafter he taught hundreds of students. Indeed, Dunn's influence may be greater as a teacher than as an artist. He himself thought so, once remarking, "Teaching is the most important work I have ever done."[13] With his students, one writer has noted, "he had Pyle's gift of instant transference—now on the firm earth beside them, speaking of homely and common things; then, off into the blue, somehow finding words to describe the indescribable." And through the years of the 1920s and the 1930s, Dunn and his pupils left a mark on American illustration, most of his students adopting "the broad-stroked dash of his oil technique. It was a school of masculine vigor, singing color, and ample design."[14] In addition, Dunn taught that there was no chasm between fine art and illustration; to him they were the same. "The Old Masters were really illustrators," he once said. Nor did he belittle advertising, observing that "American advertising art is the greatest art in the world." The reason: "The money they paid was direct and positive proof you are producing work of value and worth." He once advised students that when asked what a picture was for, one should promptly reply: "For Sale!"[15]

Throughout, however, Dunn continued his own work. He painted what he knew best, following his own dictum to students. One thing that Dunn had come to know well was war. He was obviously deeply touched by his brief but intense experiences in France. The hard truths of "man's inhumanity to man," the ravaged villages, the mud and the grime, so far removed from quiet studios, left scars and memories. Indeed, Dunn's friends and students noted something of a change in him following his return from abroad. Merely to illustrate books and magazines seemed a lesser goal now. What Dunn wanted after the war was to paint art "which could be framed to hang for posterity." But he eventually came to realize that what he knew even better than war was Dakota. "I prefer painting pictures of early South Dakota life to any other kind," he once explained, concluding that his "search for other horizons" led him back to his first horizon.[16] What came to be called Dunn's "Prairie Series" was launched, and though not the result of an organized effort, by the end of his life it consisted of many large canvases illustrating what homesteading was like in Dakota's early years. These strikingly beautiful pictures capture not only the essence of much of America's frontier experience in the Dakotas but much of Dunn's personality as well. The art reveals the boldness of its creator, as well as the harsh frontier he knew as a boy. Rich colors predominate, put on heavily without stint, his technique no doubt influenced by his encounter with the art of Vincent van Gogh in the 1930s. "That man was a color scientist," he once said with admiration.[17]

Although in the second world war Harding was disposed to go once more to the battle zone, Dunn declined, even though he was younger than his former colleague. Dunn contented himself with joining the United Service Organization (USO), traveling to military hospitals and training camps to sketch portraits of wounded soldiers, visiting with them, and swapping war stories. There were ads to illustrate for the Pepperell Company, which was too busy making uniforms to turn out bedsheets for civilians, its usual function. The Coca-Cola Company used his pictures showing servicemen enjoying that ubiquitous drink on far-flung battlefields. The White Motor Company's trucks and buses were now transporting men and matériel to war, and Dunn depicted GI's as his brushes had once painted their fathers and uncles, the doughboys of the AEF.

By the end of World War II, Dunn was no longer in much demand, either as illustrator or as teacher. Art illustration in general was in decline as photographs became more important in advertising, not to mention the arrival of television. Dunn might well have faded away altogether were it not for one development: his art began to attract considerable interest in South Dakota. Dunn's resurrection came in 1950, when he displayed forty-two of his prairie scenes at the Masonic temple in De Smet, South Dakota. The exhibition was a great success, and Dunn was so moved by the response of the people of Dakota to his art that when the show was over, on August 24, he presented a group of the paintings to the state, making the state college at Brookings its permanent custodian.[18] Officials gladly accepted the gift, and a suitable building was later erected to house Dunn's works, as well as other art. Known today as the South Dakota Memorial Art Center, it contains a fine collection of Dunn's pictures as well as his papers.[19]

Beyond this, Dunn has been honored and remembered in other ways. In 1945, he received the coveted rank of National Academician from the National Academy of Design. From 1948 to 1951, he was president of the Society of Illustrators, which named him to its Hall of Fame. On June 9, 1952, South Dakota State University conferred upon him an honorary doctor of fine arts degree. Since Dunn was by then suffering from a fatal disease, the degree was awarded in absentia. He died at his home in Tenafly, New Jersey, on October 29, 1952, but he was not forgotten. In the 1970s, the city of Brookings named a street after him. Almost a mile in length, it appropriately runs to the Memorial Art Center.

Dunn's growing reputation has been apparent in other ways. He and his art have been the subject of numerous articles. These articles usually focus on his prairie paintings and his career as teacher, though his wartime pictures have also been widely reproduced.[20] In addition, in recent years Dunn's pictures have frequently been exhibited.[21]

Harding

After the Armistice, George Harding spent a few weeks in Germany with the occupying forces. Back in France, he worked out of a studio in Paris, spending the latter part of December visiting the battlefields. Then he desired to be sent home, where his own well-appointed studio awaited him and where he could work "to best advantage and put in permanent form the impressions and sketches made at the front." He could also more easily consult with the War Department regarding what work they might have in mind for him. Harding was of a mind that the nature of his work was different from that of the other official artists and so required a different method of approach. He had paid special attention to gathering material to be used "in mural decoration and permanent painting."[22]

Following Harding's return to the United States aboard the *North Carolina*, he was discharged from the army in May of 1919, long before he could finish his planned work. Washington was plainly not interested in allowing him to paint the elaborate murals he hoped to create. But unlike Dunn, who only later completed his war pictures, Harding immediately turned to the task of salvaging his notes and field sketches. By 1920, he had produced his portfolio, *The American Expeditionary Forces in Action*, thereby ending the World War I phase of his career.

Shortly thereafter, in 1922, Harding became head of the department of illustration at the Pennsylvania Academy of the Fine Arts. He later developed and headed the mural decoration department at that school. With only a leave of absence during World War II, he remained a member of the faculty of the academy until illness forced his retirement in 1958. Also, for a number of years, Harding taught in the Fine Arts School of the University of Pennsylvania, and from the mid-1920s to 1945, he was a sometime lecturer at the Moore Institute and School of Design for Women in Philadelphia.

Harding also maintained his own studio at Wynnewood, Pennsylvania, near Philadelphia, where he lived, and nurtured his parallel career as a muralist. Many of his first mural commissions were to decorate large motion picture houses that were rapidly springing up in the 1920s, as well as banks and public buildings.[23] As a participant in the New Deal art programs in the 1930s, Harding painted murals for the Philadelphia Custom House and the North Branch Post Office in that city and, in Washington, D.C., for the United States Post Office Administration Building. In 1939 he did the gigantic mural decorating the United States Government Building at the New York World's Fair, perhaps the largest mural ever done in America (it was almost 108 feet high). Harding drew the master design one-sixth the completed size, and under his supervision a corps of trained artists did the final painting from a large scaffold.[24] In 1940 Harding decorated the Municipal Court House in Philadelphia and, in 1941, painted a mural for the Wilkes-Barre Post Office.

During World War II, as in World War I, Harding turned his talents to the service of the government. During the military buildup prior to Pearl Harbor, he joined other artists to produce a circulating art exhibition devoted to the "soldiers of production." Sponsored by the Office for Emergency Management, it was meant to stimulate interest in war production and to recognize what war workers were accomplishing. Harding's contributions were lithographic drawings of various aspects of shipbuilding.[25]

But the attack on Pearl Harbor and the U.S. entry into the war convinced Harding to seek a more active role. At the age of sixty, he accepted a commission as a captain in the U.S. Marine Corps and proceeded to the South Pacific. There he remained for twenty months, producing more than six hundred pictures, mainly in crayon and watercolor. He covered the Marine landings on Bougainville, New Georgia, Munda, and Guam, and many lesser islands. His work was done under some of the most adverse conditions of his remarkable career. "The heat was intense," he once wrote, and "sweat from my wrist often wrinkled up the paper I was doing my sketches on. The rubber bands which I used to hold the paper in rolls often came apart in the heat. When it rained, I had to cover up the whole works with a poncho, and go on sketching." As in World War I, Harding possessed an unlimited pass and could join and leave any outfit at any time. And as he had done in World War I, his system was to sketch hurriedly while under enemy fire, putting down a series of "very intimate" subjects, leaving the details for a quieter time when he could finish the work while the scenes were still fresh in his mind.[26]

Ninety-two of Harding's combat sketches were displayed even before the end of the conflict, in early 1945, at the Carnegie Institute in Pittsburgh. Later he participated with other Marine artists in a major showing of Marine Corps battle art of World War II. Held at the National Art Gallery from November 10 to December 9, 1945, it was in honor of the 170th anniversary of the U.S. Marine Corps.[27]

After the war, Harding resumed his career as a teacher and muralist. Numerous exhibitions of his art were scheduled, and he won his share of medals and awards. Perhaps most important of all was his election as National Academician by the National Academy of Design in 1945.[28] Major collections of his works are held by museums across the country, as well as by many private collectors. Felled by a stroke in 1958, Harding was forced into retirement. He died on March 26, 1959, at his home in Wynnewood.[29]

Morgan

At the end of shooting, Wallace Morgan followed the occupation forces of the AEF into Luxembourg and Germany but soon returned to Neufchâteau by way of the St. Mihiel salient and the area around Verdun. Satisfied that his field work was essentially complete, Morgan requested that he be stationed in Paris to continue his painting. Finishing his work on March 1, 1919, he was ordered to St. Aignan for embarkation processing. He was shortly in America, and a civilian again.[30]

Following his military service, Morgan continued his career as illustrator of books, articles, and stories. He made drawings for the writings of H. G. Wells, John Erskine, Damon Runyon, and Richard Harding Davis, among others, many appearing in *Collier's, Cosmopolitan,* and the *New Yorker.* In the 1930s, he illustrated stories by P. G. Wodehouse, mainly for the *Saturday Evening Post.* Appreciating Wodehouse's humor, which was rather like his own, he especially enjoyed working with the English writer. He also drew pictures for several articles by Harris Dickson on New Orleans and the shrimp fishermen of the Gulf, much as he had done earlier for Julian Street.[31]

Morgan did not neglect advertising art, his most noteworthy being a series of drawings for the Hamburg-America and North German Lloyd steamship lines. He made these drawings on shipboard while on cruises to Germany.[32]

Like several of the official artists, Morgan taught art. At various times between 1905 and 1929 he was on the faculty of the Art Students' League, at last being made an honorary member, a rare honor extended only to such artists as Pyle and George Bellows.[33]

Morgan was also closely associated with the Society of Illustrators. He was its president from 1929 to 1935 and until his death served as honorary president. While in this office, he was instrumental in acquiring and rebuilding the society's present clubhouse in Manhattan.[34]

During World War II, Morgan illustrated ads and articles on wartime themes. At the age of seventy, he served as a volunteer morale-builder in veterans' hospitals, making sketches of wounded soldiers.[35]

By the end of the war, Morgan had little of his life remaining. He died in New York City on April 24, 1948, having received many honors in the course of his life. Not only was he honorary president of the Society of Illustrators, he had also been elected to its Hall of Fame. Of the other official artists, only Dunn shared this distinction. Also like Dunn and Harding, in 1947 Morgan was elected a member of the National Academy of Design.[36]

Morgan was acclaimed by his peers, being regarded as one of the best artists in black-and-white in his time. He was often referred to as the "dean of American illustrators." As one artist put it, "Even today the camera may have an unfailing eye, but it lacks the mind and heart, the editorial report of a Wallace Morgan."[37]

Peixotto

Ernest Peixotto had witnessed the excitement of Armistice day in Paris. Back at Neufchâteau following his sojourn in the capital, Peixotto and Smith set out for Clermont-en-Argonne, Varennes, and Grandpré, sketching along the way. The two then arrived at Sedan, claiming to be perhaps the first American officers to enter it after its liberation.[38]

From Sedan, Peixotto went to Dun-sur-Meuse and Verdun, remaining at the latter for several days to sketch its ruined streets, cathedral, and the battered Bishop's Palace. On November 24, Peixotto departed for Luxembourg, traveling by way of Toul, Pont-à-Mousson, Metz, and Thionville. The Alzette Valley in Luxembourg, picturesque as ever, attracted the artist's pen, and in the little duchy he made several sketches of American troops poised to enter Germany. By the end of the month, they were prepared to move in unison with the Allies across the German border. Early in December, Peixotto followed the troops in and was soon in Coblenz, headquarters of the American occupation zone.[39]

Pausing for a brief time in Coblenz, in the early morning of December 13, 1918, the U.S. troops began to cross the Rhine on a pontoon bridge, bound for the territory allotted to them on the river's east bank. This procession went on for several days, and to all who observed it, it was an occasion to be remembered, being recognized as the culmination of the American war effort. Peixotto carefully recorded these events on canvas.[40]

Peixotto spent some time in Germany making numerous sketches, returning to Paris on December 22. He located quarters at 166 Boulevard du Montparnasse, setting up his studio at 4 bis Cité du Retiro.[41]

From late December to early February, 1918–19, Peixotto completed many of the drawings that he had begun while in the Argonne and on his trip to Germany. Then, when it appeared that he might soon be ready to accept his discharge, he was presented with an opportunity and accepted assignment to the American Expeditionary Forces' Art Training Center at the Pavillon de Bellevue, near Paris.[42] The center was part of a general educational scheme that had originally been worked out by the YMCA's Educational Commission in New York. The commission was responding to a plan to institute a considerable educational venture to provide the men of the AEF, and those with the occupation forces in Germany, with self-improving educational opportunities while they waited to return home. The plans made it possible for some doughboys to attend British and French schools, including Oxford, Cambridge, and the Sorbonne. But one of the most ambitious projects was the founding of the AEF's own University of Beaune, located in southeastern France. On April 16, 1919, the YMCA's efforts were taken over by the army when the Army Educational Corps was organized.

Those reponsible for creating the university concluded that art should be included in the curriculum. This move would make it possible for American soldiers to take advantage of the artistic and cultural wealth that abounded in France, especially in Paris. For this reason, the Pavillon de Bellevue, where Isadora Duncan had earlier held her dancing school and which was later a Red Cross hospital, was requisitioned and transformed into an art school. A faculty of forty-three men was speedily organized, and departments of interior decoration, painting, and sculpture and a division of city planning were established. Peixotto was made head of the department of painting, and he energetically assumed his duties, sometimes drawing upon the assistance of his AEF artist colleague Harry Townsend. Over three hundred students arrived for classes. However, with the rapid departure of much of the AEF for home, the university closed its doors on June 15, 1919, after only one short semester of about three months. Nevertheless, much work had been concentrated into the time available, benefiting thousands of students. One art student asserted that his "three months at Bellevue had made up for the loss of two years' work while in the Army."[43]

Following his stint at the center, Peixotto was demobilized in France, once more taking up residence at Samois-sur-Seine. One of the reasons for his decision to stay was his desire to be accredited as artist to the Paris peace conference. He attempted to obtain this position through military channels, only to learn, as Major Stone informed him, that the American Commission to Negotiate Peace was in no way associated with the army. Though Stone gave Peixotto a letter of introduction to the secretary of the American Commission, nothing came of the effort.[44]

Afterward, in 1923, though he was back in America, Peixotto became associated with the Fontainebleau School of Fine Arts, the successor of the AEF's Bellevue art school. In that year, the French government, through its Ministry of Fine Arts, transformed a wing of the Palais de Fontainebleau into studios for American art and architecture students. The palace already housed a school of music. American advanced students of art and music could now study in France for three-month terms. The school's American Committee for Art, based in the United States, was jointly headed by Whitney Warren, who represented architectural studies, and Peixotto, representing the disciplines of painting and sculpture.[45]

Following his return to the United States, Peixotto also became the director of the department of mural painting of the Beaux Arts Institute of Design in New York City. Remaining until 1926, he retired to devote the remainder of his life to mural painting, writing, and encouraging the arts in other ways.[46] He attracted much attention and gained considerable prosperity as muralist in the late 1920s and on into the 1930s, specializing in decorating the homes and villas of the affluent, especially in California and on Long Island.[47] He also decorated banks and other buildings with his murals.[48]

In the 1930s, he became a warm supporter of the Works Progress Administration's Federal Art Project, crediting it with "bringing mural painting to its true recognition," asserting that the masses in America were being artistically stirred as never before. He also painted murals for New Deal art programs. In 1935, Mayor La Guardia made Peixotto a member of the New York City Municipal Art Commission to coordinate federal and city art projects, a post he held until January 18, 1940. In addition, he served as consultant on murals for the New York World's Fair organization. He died suddenly of a coronary thrombosis on December 6, 1940, at the age of seventy-one.[49]

Smith   As with the other artists, J. André Smith followed the American troops to Germany, staying until late December, 1918. He then took up his residence at 22 Rue Ponthieu in Paris, where he undertook to complete his etchings and lithographs.[50] However, completing the projects took longer than he had anticipated. By January of 1919 he had finished 194 pictures for the army and requested that he be allowed to go home sometime between mid-February and the first of March.[51] But he then decided to join Capt. Joseph Mills Hanson, of *Stars and Stripes*, on a tour of the British and Belgian fronts where some Americans had served during the war. "I had always hoped to be able to cover this part of our fighting and the chance to go . . . seemed too valuable to refuse," he wrote. Only after this venture did Smith return home. He was discharged from the army in April of 1919.[52]

Shortly after Smith's return to civilian life he published *In France with the American Expeditionary Forces*, which consisted of one hundred of his selected drawings, showing, as he stated it, "as nearly as possible, our various Army activities that came to my notice during the year in which I served with the A.E.F." Observing that his drawings depicted only the "background of the A.E.F.," he advised "the searcher after sensational pictures of conflict, the horrors of war, and the anecdotic record of soldier life and heroism" to look elsewhere. The war posed for him, he insisted, rather as "a very deliberate worker who goes about his task of fighting in a methodical and thorough manner," and "if the picture of war which the sum total of my drawings shows has any virtue of truth or novelty it is in this respect: It shows War, the business man, instead of War, the warrior. It is an unsensational record of things actually seen, and in almost every instance drawn . . . 'on the spot.'"[53] Smith would have none of the heroics of war and its destruction. It had become only a business—a dirty business—which the designer, architect, and expressionist etcher, did not wish to exalt. The book brought Smith's war art to a larger public and helped launch his postwar freelance artistic career.

By this time, Smith had moved from New York City to Stony Creek, Connecticut, where he maintained a residence until his death. Continuing to etch, he branched out in his work, becoming a muralist and stage set designer.[54] From 1922 to 1924, he designed sets for the Parish Players in Stony Creek and later published a book, *The Scenewright*, which for years was widely used as a textbook.[55]

At this juncture, Smith suffered a personal crisis. While in officer's training in 1917, at Plattsburg, he had injured his right leg on a strand of barbed wire. It did not heal properly. Much later, in 1924, a massive embolism developed in the leg, which had to be amputated above the knee. When complications developed, further operations became necessary. Smith suffered the remainder of his life from "phantom pain," which seems to come from the severed limb. It was many months before he could resume serious artistic activity.[56]

When Smith's health permitted, he reinstituted his European travels, and from 1925 to 1930, largely financed by money inherited from his father, Smith was able to winter in southern France. There he experimented in art, his paintings, watercolors, and etchings inspired by diverse European artists ranging from Van Gogh,

Utrillo, and Cézanne to Braque and Picasso and varying from literalism to expressionism, from somber tones to the use of bright, dazzling colors.[57]

In the early 1930s, religious themes began to appear in Smith's work, and in both paintings and sculpture he did his share of Madonnas and Crucifixions. Later in the decade, he experimented with "automatic painting," which resulted in a remarkable book, *Art and the Subconscious*, published in 1937 and touted as "an important contribution both to art and psychology." The book, five hundred copies of which were published privately, was "a record of an experience in psychical transcription, whereby through a complete resignation of the conscious mind, rather than by the usual means of deliberate mental concentration this series of remarkable drawings here reproduced came into existence." The book was given a mixed reception.[58]

More importantly, in the 1930s Smith became attracted to Winter Park, Florida. There he met Mary Louise Curtis Bok, the widow of noted Philadelphia philanthropist Edward Bok. Becoming an admirer of Smith and his work, in 1936 Mary Bok offered to build a gallery to house and display his paintings and sculptures. Smith responded by proposing that an art center be created where visiting artists could study and explore experimental techniques under his direction. Readily agreeing, Mary Bok purchased land in Maitland, Florida, in 1937 for the Research Studio, as the art center would be called.[59]

Formally opened in January of 1938, the studio was expanded over the next several years, emerging as a complex of buildings consisting of studios, galleries, courtyards, gardens, artists' quarters, a library, and related structures, to which was added an open-air chapel in 1942. The facility became a work of art in itself, one of the "important examples of fantastic architecture in America."[60]

Smith saw the Research Studio as a place for work, rest, and contemplation, in keeping with his views that "a man does more when he seems to be doing less. Ideas come to him not in the tumult of activity but in the silence of relaxed contemplation. In such a mood of mental tranquility a man becomes 'detached,' he rises above his material surroundings into a spiritual consciousness."[61] In short, Smith's creation was an "art monastery."

Smith hoped to help other artists to produce great artworks in the surroundings of the studio. The first year he invited five artists to take up fellowships, providing them with self-contained, separate living quarters, free communal meals, and art supplies, as well as his own supervision and encouragement. World War II interrupted the studio's activities; there were no guest artists in residence from 1943 to 1945. After the war, to the time of Smith's death, artists once more worked with him. In all, about sixty artists resided at the studio during Smith's lifetime.[62]

Smith's absorption in his work steadily produced results. He continued to paint and draw, though worsening eyesight precluded his etching by the mid-1930s. His works to the end bore the marks of experimentation. He left behind thousands of pictures when he died from heart failure on March 3, 1959, at age seventy-eight. He was buried, not in Florida, but at Branford, Connecticut, near his permanent home at Stony Creek.[63]

For a decade following Smith's death, there was much uncertainty as to the future of the Research Studio. Mary Bok, by then married to Efrem Zimbalist, Sr., no longer supported it. For a time it was kept going, but in 1962, the Research Studio was merged with the Central Florida Museum (now the Loch Haven Art Center). In 1964, the museum announced plans to close the studio and sell it. This action was blocked by concerned artists, and in 1966 the City of Maitland agreed to buy the studio. Legal problems arose, however, and it was not until 1969 that Maitland took possession of it. Between 1964 and 1969, Smith's studio was abandoned, given up to the ravages of vandals, rot, weeds, and the weather. Steady progress was made in restoring it, and in 1971 the Maitland Art Association placed the Maitland Art Center, as the old studio is now called, into operation. In 1982, it was entered on both the state register and National Register of Historic Places, its future perhaps secured. It now offers year-round classes and workshops for both children and adults, with professional staff artists placing emphasis on individual instruction and student development. Advanced students are encouraged to pursue experimental approaches to art; Smith would no doubt approve. In addition, exhibitions, lectures, concerts, and dance recitals are held frequently, and an annual jazz festival is presented. Thus, as intended by Smith, "the Maitland Art Center is a dynamic institution where art, artists, and the public interact." It is, in addition, "a perpetual memorial to its founder, . . . who believed art to be a constantly changing reflection of the present time rooted deeply in the events of the past."[64]

Townsend

As with the other artists, following his trip to the occupation zone in Germany, Harry Townsend left Neufchâteau. He obtained a studio at 4 Rue Belloni in Paris, moving in on January 12, 1919. Beginning work soon thereafter, he planned several trips to the old battlefields as soon as the spring weather permitted.[65]

At this point, other opportunities arose. Townsend succeeded in being accredited to the Paris peace conference—where Peixotto had failed. For a brief time before he sailed home he attended several sessions, making interesting sketches of many of the statesmen assembled for the negotiations.[66] He was also able to assist

Peixotto at the Pavillon de Bellevue, especially with the students who were study-ing poster art.

He then visited the battlefields as he had long planned, but these efforts did not pay off as he intended because of incessant rain and cold. He therefore asked for orders home. These were soon forthcoming, and Townsend sailed from Le Havre on May 24. He was discharged from the army on June 3.[67]

Unlike Dunn, Harding, and some of the other artists, Townsend did little with combat art in later years. He became involved in his own pursuit of "normalcy." Reestablishing himself in New York, he and his family shortly thereafter, in 1921, moved to Connecticut, that state being by then a center of considerable artistic and cultural activity. The Townsends chose Norwalk as their home, and, buying an old barn, they transformed it into a showplace home and studio.

Townsend rapidly established himself on the Connecticut artistic scene. He was a charter member of the influential Silvermine Guild of Artists, founded in 1922 in New Canaan, serving on its board for the remainder of his life and as its president for 1926–27. He was active in the Westport Artists' Market and partici-pated in numerous exhibitions of the era. He continued to instruct in art, for the Silvermine Guild, for example, and conducted classes at his studio in Norwalk.[68]

Townsend died on July 25, 1941, at his Norwalk home.[69] He was survived by his widow and fellow artist Cory, and his daughter Barbara, who became a writer on art and a watercolor artist. For a time, she was on the staff of the Museum of Modern Art in New York.

5. The Fruits of Their Labor

Although the U.S. Army did not discharge all of the artists at the same time, the general policy was to expedite their removal from the service. The work that the artists managed to complete before becoming civilians would be transmitted to the War Department. Other works, sketches, and field notes yet to be completed could later be purchased by the War Department, if it so desired, or would remain the property of the artists.[1] The results produced a mixed legacy. Some artwork became the property of the U.S. government; much remained in the hands of the artists.

In the meantime, the U.S. Army seemed as eager to divest itself of the art as it had been to discharge its creators. Pleading that the army was not the proper custodian of works of art and emphasizing that it did not have the facilities to care for and exhibit them, the General Staff decided that another "permanent repository of these productions is . . . desirable in order that they may be available for the inspection of the greatest number."[2] The logical agency to take over the art was the United States National Museum, part of the Smithsonian Institution. Accordingly, on July 19, 1919, Colonel Weeks at the War Department contacted the executive secretary of the museum, W. de C. Ravenel, who promptly accepted the offer, observing however, that the museum would "of course, never be able to place them all on exhibition at the same time, but . . . will be able no doubt to show all of those of special interest."[3] This dashed the hopes of the artists that all of their work might be placed on permanent public display, but it set forth the policy of the Smithsonian Institution that still exists regarding the official art of the AEF: the institution is willing, under the usual careful controls, to lend works from the collection to art museums and other institutions and agencies. In addition, for some years immediately after the war, many of the works were prominently displayed as part of the elaborate war trophies exhibits that the Smithsonian maintained in Washington. In the Natural History Building on the Mall, a large showing of navy war trophies was in place, while the army exhibits were located in the Arts and Industries Building near the institution's famous castle on the Mall.

The army formally delivered the art to the Smithsonian Institution on January 28, 1920. The catalog that accompanied the pictures listed 497 separate pieces, to which were later added a few additional items for a total of 507 works, including one poster by Dunn, not originally a part of the collection, entitled *Victory Is a Question of Stamina*, painted for the U.S. Food Administration in 1917.[4] The collection was at first assigned to the Division of History, of what is today the National Museum of American History of the Smithsonian. Thirty-one of the pieces, pertaining to port facilities and shipping activities, were then placed in the custody of the Division of Naval History, while the others were subsequently transferred to the Division of Military History. These works constitute the official collection of the World War I combat art.

As for the works not turned over to the War Department, their locations are varied or unknown. Harvey Dunn's *Crossing a Pontoon Bridge* was purchased by the South Dakota Memorial Art Center from a private collector in 1980. Other war pieces completed by Dunn after his discharge from the army have not been located.

The New Britain Museum of American Art, New Britain, Connecticut, possesses a folder containing approximately 245 sketches and other pictures of war scenes by Townsend, many of which are incomplete.

Harding published some of the pieces that he completed after his discharge in a limited-edition portfolio of thirty-eight pictures entitled *The American Expeditionary Forces in Action*. Simultaneously, the original paintings toured as a one-man show, opening in February, 1920, at the Art Club Gallery in Philadelphia. Under the auspices of the American Federation of Arts, the exhibition then toured the country, generating a positive response in the press and from critics. The final disposition of the thirty-eight works is not known, but the U.S. Army Art Collection in 1984 purchased a group of twenty-two originals by Harding, which may include some of the thirty-eight pictures.

The U.S. Army Art Collection also purchased nineteen works in 1977 from the estate of J. André Smith and in the following year bought another 158 of his pictures. This collection of 177 pieces is composed of works that Smith apparently completed after his discharge or for some reason did not turn over to the army while he was on active service. Smith also published a collection of a hundred examples of his art in his book *In France with the American Expeditionary Forces*.

There are no doubt other works of the official artists scattered about the world, but the collection at the Smithsonian and the additions to the U.S. Army Art Collection include a large portion of what the artists produced as a consequence of their involvement as official artists of the AEF, while on active duty or after their return to private life.

Especially in later years, numerous shows and exhibitions have made use of the AEF art collection. And almost immediately, in October of 1919, the *American Legion Weekly* made reproductions of eleven of the pictures. But few people were interested in war art in the 1920s and early 1930s. It was not until war clouds once again appeared that new requests for the art were made. In 1939, the Los Angeles Museum of History, Science, and Art used eight of the works by Smith and Duncan for an exhibition. In the midst of World War II, Archibald MacLeish, the Librarian of Congress, wanted twenty-one drawings to be included in an exhibition of American battle art which opened on July 4, 1944.[5] But interest continued beyond World War II, and in 1970–71, twenty-seven of the pieces were on display at the U.S. Army Military History Research Collection (now the U.S. Army Military History Institute), Carlisle Barracks, Pennsylvania. Eighteen pictures were sent to the Brandywine Art Exhibit at Chadds Ford, Pennsylvania, June 4 to September 6, 1976; seven works enhanced a Marine Corps Museum art exhibition at the Washington Navy Yard from October 15, 1976, to May 1, 1977. The Smithsonian Institution, from April 17 to June 27, 1967, exhibited forty-six selections at the Museum of History and Technology.

The popularity and growing fame of Harvey Dunn led to several showings of his World War I art. The Brandywine River Museum borrowed thirteen paintings from the Smithsonian Institution for a show that ran from August 26, to December 6, 1974. The South Dakota Memorial Art Center, in an exhibition entitled, "Harvey Dunn: Son of the Middle Border," on display from April 1 to May 27, 1984, used several of Dunn's AEF pieces. One of Dunn's World War I scenes, *The Battle of the Marne,* a charcoal done in 1918, was the basis for a twenty-two-cent commemorative stamp released by the United States Postal Service in 1985, as part of a series honoring the nation's war veterans.

Other uses have been made of the art. Various magazines and books have used some of the works as illustrations. For example, the American Heritage publishing house used many of the pictures in the *American Heritage History of World War I.*[6] Therefore, the battle art of the AEF has not been totally forgotten and unused, even though it has not been placed on permanent public display.

As to that art, the artists inevitably concentrated on several topics pertaining to the AEF, including the activities of the base ports, and extending from there to the front. For instance, Aylward's expertise in marine art suggested that he would choose to paint scenes having to do with the activities at the ports. One of the striking features of U.S. involvement in France was the rapid expansion of port and transportation facilities undertaken by American engineers. Coming after the Armistice, Aylward's paintings were intended to create a permanent historical record of these aspects of the American war effort. Selecting the French Mediterranean port of Marseilles as his main venue for this painting, though he did some work at other sites, Aylward produced some beautiful art. The details of key activities of the Services of Supply are hereby preserved. It is obvious that Aylward was in his element. Having more leisure to paint following the end of hostilities, he lavished both time and attention on these scenes, and his *Water Front, Old Harbor, Marseilles* [A1], might have been set at any time or place in the recent past. It is vintage Aylward, reminding the viewer of many works that he had executed earlier in his career. Other canvases record typical activities centered on the ports, such as *Schooners in the Old Harbor, Marseilles* [A2] and *Repairing a Damaged Ship* [A3].

One of the noteworthy activities of the Services of Supply and the engineering troops was the bringing in of locomotives. The French were short of engines, as well as rolling stock, and the Americans greatly assisted them by supplying their own trains. The men took great pride in their ability to get locomotives quickly unloaded from the ships and, as soon as steam was up, as speedily placed into service. Duncan's pencil sketch, *Baldwin Locomotives Unloaded as Shipped on the Wharf at Brest* [B4], illustrates these successful operations.

Another characteristic activity conducted behind the lines involved the training operations of the aviators and the large flying fields constructed for the purpose. Smith, in his *Flying Field at Issoudun* [G7], created a panoramic view of the huge complex of flying fields maintained by the U.S. Army Air Services at that location.

Smith, the architect and etcher of the group, was perhaps best equipped to produce detailed studies of buildings. His excellent drawings, *Chaumont American Headquarters* [G1] and *A View of Neufchâteau* [G2], provide the student of World War I with details of the surroundings of the high command of the AEF, and the artists' base of operations. No artist of the AEF better portrayed other buildings familiar to the troops in France. The picture entitled *A Gateway to the Front, Rambucourt* [G3], in the Toul Sector, reveals the settings of mundane, day-to-day activity, also familiar to the men. The subject of housing also attracted Duncan's attention. Early in the deployment of the AEF, housing was a serious problem. Billeting officers often had to take what accommodations were immediately available. Duncan, in his drawing *Cold Nights Coming On* [B5], focuses on this state of affairs. The winter of 1917–18 was especially cold, and if one's billet was in a drafty French barn, the comforts were few, and sleep would no doubt have been elusive.

It must have pained Smith, the architect, to view countless damaged and destroyed buildings. However, he did not shrink from portraying them, and in his *Pathway to Peace* [G5] and *Flirey* [G4] he emphasizes how troops had to relate to the shattered remains of once grand buildings. Peixotto was also sensitive to these matters, no doubt because he had known France intimately before the war. He, too, was struck by the monumental ruins in the St. Mihiel area, and it is interesting to compare his *Flirey* [F1] with that of Smith, whose harder line of rectitude contrasts with Peixotto's more impressionistic treatment. Peixotto's *Troops Leaving Esnes* [F2] directs attention to the ruins that he saw in the Meuse-Argonne sector. In this work, Peixotto contrasted the living men with the devastated buildings, though the living are endowed with the heaviness of the destroyed habitations. War makes ruins of both buildings and men, so this picture suggests.

There is perhaps only so much an artist can do with ruins. Smith, in his *Pathway to Peace* [G5], turns preacher, indicating that only beyond the ruins of war, including churches and cathedrals, which seem to have failed humankind, could peace be found. Still, Smith's focus on a still-standing statue of Christ in a church suggests that even in the midst of destruction the Savior remains a symbol of peace. Significantly, it is the armed men who would bring peace. In this quest, "God has no hands but our hands; no rifles but our own," seems to be one lesson that Smith seeks to teach. Another interpretation might be that it is specifically American arms that will turn the trick. Another part of the picture emphasizes that, though the crosses that proudly adorned the structure now stand askew, they still tended to the upright amid the rubble. Numerous observers have reflected on various "miracles" pertaining to churches and cathedrals and the symbols of the Christian faith that they contain. These often absorbed great punishment in bombardments but still appeared intact. Famous examples included the unharmed crucifix in the midst of the total ruins of the church of Lucy-le-Bocage, near Belleau Wood. Another was the stone statue of the Virgin in the tower of the church of Notre Dame-Brebières in Albert, on the banks of the Ancre River in the Somme valley. These "miracles" and others were the subjects of much comment and awe. In addition to his *Pathway to Peace,* Smith further commented on these matters in his *On the Edge of Rambucourt* [G6]. This featured the shattered structure of a church which still stood as an imposing reminder of the faith that it was built to glorify.

One of the striking features of France often remarked upon is the white, tree-lined roads. But these could quickly be turned into equally striking ruins, both the roads and the trees. Numerous artists and illustrators have made studies of such scenes. The violated trees, blasted into stumps or forlorn trunks, and the churned-up roads delineate the familiar aspects of wartorn landscapes. Peixotto's *No Man's Land, near Thiaucourt* [F3], in the St. Mihiel Sector, stands with British painter Paul Nash's *The Menin Road* in defining the essence of war zone destruction in World War I.

The agents of destruction were the new instruments and engines of war so characteristic of the struggle. Harding was one of the official AEF artists who focused on the weaponry, principally tanks and aircraft. His *Tanks Attacking Early Sept. 26th between Avocourt and Montfaucon* [D1] and his *Vanquished by the Boche Plane* [D2] are examples. Dunn's *Tanks at Seichprey* [sic] [C9] was an impressionistic scene of action in the St. Mihiel campaign. Dunn emphasizes that tanks were used in support of infantry, which, despite the development of technology, remained the "Queen of Battles." Townsend also did several studies of tanks. His *The Light Tank in Action* [H3], *A Tank Surprises and Cleans Up* [H1], and *A Six-Ton Camouflaged Tank* [H2] are models of clarity. His aircraft are less distinctive, though he had an even greater interest in them. His *The Alert Nieuports* [H4] is an ethereal impression; *A Forced Landing near Neufchâteau* [H5] pictures the airmen larger than life beside their wrecked machine, which resembles an injured beetle.

There is little doubt that artillery was a most important feature of the war. It was largely responsible for the appalling casualties that the warring nations sustained and for creating the characteristic "moonscape" aspect of the zones of intense combat. Among the artillery, few weapons in history have attracted as much attention as the reliable, accurate, rapid-fire French field piece, the highly regarded, greatly venerated "75." This three-inch weapon equipped many American artillery batteries. Its exploits have been commemorated in literature, letters, memoirs, and art, and Duncan's sketch, *A Battery of French 75's Shelling the Germans on the Ridge to the Left of Château-Thierry* [B6], adds to that body of work. While not as realistic as Duncan's artillery studies, Harding's ghostly guns in *American Gun Fire Early Morning Opening Verdun Offensive* [D5], shooting out of the mists and their self-created fog of smoke, evoke in his characteristic impressionistic style a sense of the drama of a barrage. This particular cannonade, which opened the Verdun offensive in October of 1918, contributed to the coming of the Armistice a few weeks later. Significantly, the men who served these machines of destruction appear on the periphery, dwarfed by their massive charges. In the foreground, troops await the lifting of the shelling before advancing. In another study of this theme, *Verdun Offensive: American Troops Following Barrage* [D6], the victorious Americans, also supported by tanks, roll over their stunned foes, who nevertheless remain able to hurl grenades at the advancing American troops. In the picture *In Pursuit of the Enemy: American Troops Entering Village during Advance across the Marne* [D7], Harding portrays Americans on the offensive earlier in the war. It is apparent that Harding was attempting to respond to the demands of the Washington critics for more action pictures. He has crammed much activity into this canvas.

The varied activities of the rank and file attracted much attention from the artists. Of interest was the preparation of food. Aylward, in his pastel of the *First Division Headquarters Kitchen—St. Mihiel Drive* [A4], emphasized the rude surroundings in which the troops' chow was usually prepared. However, the detested "slum" (short for slumgullion, a stew), "monkey meat" (one of several canned meats), and "gold fish" (salmon) were perhaps not fit to be cooked in happier surroundings; they would have been deplored no matter where served. Harding's *Morning Mess, Beaumont-Toul Sector* [D9] was his first work as official artist and depicts the men in a lighter frame of mind. To him, chow time was not an ordeal, and for a moment military service did not appear unrelentingly harsh, bleak, and somber. Morgan's contribution to the subject, *A Cold Breakfast on the March* [E1], is rather unrealistic with its stilted, elfin-faced soldiers slogging on their way or riding on stoical, long-suffering mules, bound for somewhere.

Other dimensions of the activities of the men in the ranks were recorded. Duncan, in his *Blacksmith and Wagon Repair Shed on the Road to Boucq* [B1], reminds us that much prosaic work was involved in fighting even a modern war. There were also the unsung ambulance and truck drivers, experts in the new modes of transport now familiar if not omnipresent. As to the ambulances, adventuresome Americans had driven these since the outbreak of hostilities in 1914, long before their homeland formally entered the conflict. Duncan's pencil and ink sketch, *Awaiting a Call: French Auto Truck and Ambulances, Parked in the Place Carrière, Neufchâteau* [B2], illustrates details of this side of modern warfare. Nor were men of the medical department forgotten. Duncan pays them respects in his *Barber Shop and First-Aid Station of the Red Cross at Essey* [B3], near Nancy in the Toul Sector.

Morgan could also reveal the lighter side of the war. His *The Morning Washup, Neufmaison* [E5] is a cartoon-like rendition of a scene centered on a village pump and watering tank where horses are watered, household water drawn, teeth brushed, and men sponge-bathed, all at the same time. Here Americans and French are drawn together in a sense of friendship and alliance at a basic, homey level. There is little standing on ceremony in this quaint scene.

There were not too many Marines engaged in action in World War I, but army troops often complained that those who were hogged the glory and the headlines. Their complaints were to a degree justified. Several of the artists were attracted to the leathernecks. Morgan was one of these, spending some time with the 5th

Marine Brigade attached to the 2d Division. His scene, *Dugouts of the 5th Marines in Bois de Belleau* [E3] rather impressionistically reveals the essential details of an encampment at the front as it truly was. Another impressionistic study is the charcoal of the *Supply Trains on the Paris-Metz Road during the Battle of Belleau Wood, June 6, 1918* [E4]. Though the Americans often failed to develop orderly supply columns, the one Morgan saw in June of 1918 seems a model of organization. The supply troops are proceeding to the front with order and decorum, and a measure of efficiency, and the steady progress of the men will surely get the supplies to the front on time.

Men in movement appealed to Morgan. He was particularly interested in columns of troops. His *Machine Gun Outfit Moving Forward near Esnes during the Artillery Attack, Sept. 26* [E6] is one such study, also directing attention to the role that draft animals played in the war. The engineering troops certainly employed many horses and mules and worked them closely with the men in road building, for example. Morgan's *Engineers Building Roads* [E7] also captures the ant-like intensity of these troops at work. There is a sense of persistent inevitability about their activity; one is convinced that the road will be built.

The artists developed insights into what kind of impact the war had on the lives of the men involved. Surely there were few more stressful situations than preparing to advance into action. Nevertheless, outwardly, the men were not expected to show undue concern. If they had marched for some time prior to their being engaged, their nonchalance would have been conditioned by fatigue. Certainly Aylward's *Troops Waiting to Advance at Hattonchâtel, St. Mihiel Drive* [A5] seem hardly filled with anxiety. They reveal more accurately the adage about military life: "Hurry up and wait." Compositionally, the picture is of interest. The arch forces attention on the troops much as a telescope lens would. Whatever their demeanor, the men are calmly awaiting their fate. Here they were participating in America's first major operation of the war—the successful action at St. Mihiel.

But fatigue was a problem. Tired men attracted Morgan's attention, and his sympathy for them is clearly revealed in his *American Artillery Relieved at Deumx after Days of Hard Fighting* [E2]. He successfully mirrors the troops' awful weariness and gives a graphic view of tired crusaders engaged in "making the world safe for democracy." If not suffering as Washington's men did at Valley Forge, they have nonetheless been temporarily drained of élan, of "prunes and glory." The soldiers, having reached the region of undestroyed trees, can now look forward perhaps to some well-earned repose. They will return to fight another day.

Dunn's works perhaps best captured the impact of war on the fighting man. In his *Off Duty* [C1] Dunn strongly evokes the deep fatigue that penetrated to the very marrow of the bones of frontline troops. The two doughboys in the picture do not expect much. Indeed, they are relieved to have a few minutes to themselves to smoke and to read a paper, perhaps from home, weeks old, or a copy of the *Stars and Stripes*. Yet the men are ready to spring into action, or at least painfully to bestir themselves again. The rifle is well within grasp, the helmets are near at hand or kept on the head; the gas masks are nearby. The men expect within a short time to shoulder their burdens and once more return to the conflict.

Another study of a different sort of respite, Dunn's *In the Front Line at Early Morning* [C2], has captured the essence of an even deeper fatigue. The soldier awaits a possible enemy attack and will sound the alarm at the first hint of danger. His own issue grenades are ready at hand, together with two captured German "potato masher" grenades; the rifle is obviously loaded, the bayonet already fixed; the gas mask is ready for instant use if the gas gong sounds. Yet the man has had little rest during the night and perhaps for the past several days. One can only hope that his ordeal will soon end and he will be able to get the sleep that his whole body cries out for.

Doughboys often cursed the heavy packs that they had to wear. Dunn sympathized with the men, who normally carried up to seventy pounds or more and an eight-pound rifle as well as a heavy overcoat and a helmet, which was heavier than it looked and tired out the neck muscles. There were, too, the mud-caked boots to drag around. In the almost caricature-like *The Engineer* [C3], Dunn graphically reveals the doughboy as beast of burden.

Yet not all of the men were crushed by their equipment. The figure in Dunn's *The Machine Gunner* [C4] was clearly in his element. He wears his accoutrements with an air of easy nonchalance. He is obviously in charge of his situation, a man master of himself and of others under his command and unafraid of the enemy or anything that fate might have in store for him. War not only crushes and destroys; it also brings out the heroic in those strong enough to meet its demands. Dunn understood something of the nature and magnitude of that challenge.

Nevertheless, the harshness of World War I, with its impersonal technology and destruction, was capable of destroying the bravest of the brave. No man's land remains the final word on the destructive capabilities of modern weapons, and even aviators, soaring above the conflict, could be snatched down and forced into the mud and filth of the fields of protracted battle. Dunn's charcoal, *No Mans Land* [C5], is a graphic illustration of the war's great destruction in which men, machines, and beasts of burden alike were consumed. This theme greatly attracted Dunn, and he made various studies of the front, the haunting, moaning locale so often evoked by veterans who had been there. *The Harvest Moon* [C6] is a parody of a usually benign phenomenon familiar to rural Americans; the brilliant moon of autumn whose light usually shone upon bountiful harvests. American farm boys, as the fall of 1918 approached, anticipated harvests of another kind. The metaphor of battle as harvest was one that struck many doughboys. In Dunn's *The Flare* [C7], manufactured pyrotechnics substitute for the moon, but the eerie artificial light reveals a macabre harvest. The color-charcoal work entitled *The Hand Grenade* [C8] indicates how that harvest was brought in.

The men who had been through battle were subjects sought by the artists. Aylward presents a thoughtful solitary doughboy in his study entitled *His Bunkie* [A6]. The soldier is contemplating the cost of war in personal terms, as it has robbed him of his buddy, who up to that shattering time had shared the boredom, fears, and excitement of service in France. The companionship felt by military men is proverbial, and Americans shared this to the fullest. Townsend's thoughtful *Infantryman* [H9] is a study of the quiet strength of an American doughboy, little bowed down by his heavy equipment, which he easily shoulders. But this soldier has no doubt lost some of his earlier idealism. While plainly determined to see the job through, this pensive man has matured and been sobered by active service and the responsibility of his sergeant's stripes.

Townsend understood as well as any of the artists did the tendency of the war experience to force foot soldiers to become part of the mud through which they slogged. Whether of the German or Allied armies, the rank and file appear similar, with only the differences in uniforms and equipment differentiating them. A series of Townsend's studies elaborated on these matters. These studies include *On the Gas Alert* [H6] and *Soldiers of the Telephone* [H7]. His charcoal sketch entitled *Helping a Wounded Ally* [H8] is a metaphor for the American involvement in the war. As such, it features an American soldier carrying a wounded French *poilu*, and not the other way around.

Dunn was also keenly aware that war did not draw distinctions among men. They were forced into a common mold, friend and foe alike, and when German prisoners were pressed into service as stretcher bearers, as Dunn presents them in his *Prisoners and Wounded* [C10], the helmets and uniforms seem their sole distinguishing mark. Harding's views of wounded men were also imbued with provocative aspects of suffering humanity and commentary on the leveling aspects of war. In his pictures *Verdun Offensive: Wounded Working Back to Advanced Aid Station* [D3] and *First Aid Station with American Wounded Carried in by Boche Prisoners Early in Verdun Offensive* [D4] both the American wounded and German prisoners are pressed into service as stretcher bearers, revealing that war defeats both sides engaged. Assuredly, Harding tells us, there are no winners—only victims.

Dunn did recognize losers, however. His *Kamerad—The Sniper* [C11] reveals a hard-faced foe, but one now vanquished and ready to obey the orders of his captors. However, in *The Boche Looter* [C12] Dunn delineates all of the harsh aspects of the unrepentant enemy—the perennial Hun—the subjection of which was the prime cause of America's involvement in the struggle. The looter's helmet makes him appear to be a rapacious beetle, scuttling off with his ill-gotten gains. He is certainly an antagonist to be relentlessly destroyed, one to whom no quarter could be given. Nevertheless, Americans, long famous as inveterate souvenir hunters, often availed themselves of loot. Harding's study, *To the Victor Belong the Spoils* [D8], illustrates the sorts of booty that would have attracted the men. The soldier at the center of the picture has overloaded himself. One wonders whether he will be able to keep all the items that he has "liberated." When he tires, he will no doubt jettison some of his gains, if not parts of his regulation equipment instead. The soldier who has adorned himself with a German steel helmet will no doubt speedily take it off during the next engagement, as the silhouette that he presents will make him a target of Allied guns.

If the artists reflected on the leveling aspects of the war regarding the soldiers, they did not ignore other poignant scenes such as the refugees—the flotsam and jetsam of modern warfare. The vast scale of military operations in recent times has vastly multiplied the numbers of civilians involved. World War I produced its millions of despairing dispossessed. Aylward was among those observers who has recorded their plight. His *Refugees Returning to Their Homes—Hattonchâtel* [A7] is a fitting counterpoint to the American troops waiting to advance in the same locale, Hattonchâtel, which Aylward also painted [A5]. Both groups had been assembled by the whims of war, and it is symptomatic of that strife that both refugee and soldier reflect some of the same stoic resignation that the surroundings and circumstances forced upon them.

From the Allied point of view, the war resulted in vistas of victory as well. Peixotto for one produced several works recording some of these. One was the occasion when General Pershing entered St. Mihiel, following the successful conclusion of the AEF's first major campaign. Peixotto, who was present, described the incident in detail in his account of the war, *The American Front*. He made a charcoal of the scene for the pictorial record as well. His *General Pershing Entering St. Mihiel* [F4] depicts troops in dress formation flanked by a dense group of civilians with Pershing in the center. The date of this event, September 13, 1918, remained for Peixotto one of the memorable days in the history of the AEF.

Another study in victory by Peixotto is the charcoal, *German Shelters near Varennes* [F5]. This featured billets used by the Germans before their defeat in the Argonne. Many of the shelters were intact, though the destruction of major buildings is also faithfully recorded. That there were casualties in the operation that led to their capture is evidenced by a small grouping of crosses near one of the structures, though whether they mark the graves of Germans or Americans is not clear.

But the end of the war was the most satisfying victory of all. Peixotto shared with his fellow artists an extensive trip into the American zone of occupation following the end of hostilities. The route taken by the American troops to their area was through Luxembourg and along the Moselle River to Coblenz, the major German city at the confluence of the Moselle and the Rhine which had been designated the headquarters of the American zone. Though some of the American troops rode into Germany, the vast majority marched the two hundred miles or more from their French bases.

The troops of the famed 1st Division established themselves at Montabaur and other German towns. Peixotto drew a scene of this picturesque German town, entitling it *Main Square, Montabaur, Headquarters of the 1st Division* [F6]. For many months the goals of the American troops were the Rhine and Berlin. They were not destined to reach the German capital, but they were, much sooner than many expected, to see the German Rhine of story and legend. Peixotto captured something of what this meant in his *Boppard on the Rhine in the American Sector* [F7], a picture postcard view familiar to many American troops. More dramatic is the artist's *First Americans Crossing the Rhine* [F8], which directs attention to an event that began on December 13, 1918. For several days thereafter, American troops, bound for several bases beyond the Rhine to the east, marched across the river using the pontoon bridge at Coblenz. Townsend also captures something of the drama of the American occupation in his study, *Our Troops Entering Coblenz* [H10].

In the last analysis, despite the disagreements that surfaced about the art of the official AEF artists, a respectable body of work was created, both as to quantity and quality. Though unprepared to immediately assume their duties upon their arrival in France, the men rapidly familiarized themselves with the war's demands upon them as artists. Drawing upon their skills as illustrators, and often accustomed to working within deadlines, they were soon creating respectable pictures. If not initially acceptable to critics at the War Department, the art passed the sharp scrutiny of veterans within the AEF, and with the refinements soon evident, even Washington agreed that the work was adequate if not exceptional.

Not used or exhibited as it might have been subsequently, the artistic record that the official artists produced remains a part of America's cultural heritage and its long tradition of battle art. Worthy of serious study, it is also worth viewing for its own sake and an appreciation of its frequently striking qualities as a visual record of America's involvement in the Great War.

Part II. The Artists' Images

Water Front, Old Harbor, Marseilles, W. J. Aylward, March, 1919, watercolor
(*National Archives*)

A1

Schooners in the Old Harbor, Marseilles, W. J. Aylward, March, 1919, watercolor (*National Archives*)

A2

Repairing a Damaged Ship, W. J. Aylward, March, 1919, watercolor (*National Archives*)

A3

First Division Headquarters Kitchen—St. Mihiel Drive, W. J. Aylward, October, 1918, pastel (*Smithsonian Institution*)

A4

A5

Troops Waiting to Advance at Hattonchâtel, St. Mihiel Drive, W. J. Aylward, October, 1918, oil (*Smithsonian Institution*)

His Bunkie, W. J. Aylward, July, 1918, watercolor (*Smithsonian Institution*)

A6

Refugees Returning to Their Homes—Hattonchâtel, W. J. Aylward, September, 1918, watercolor (*Smithsonian Institution*)

A7

Blacksmith and Wagon Repair Shed on the Road to Boucq, W. J. Duncan, May 20, 1918, pencil sketch (*Smithsonian Institution*)

B1

Awaiting a Call: French Auto Truck and Ambulances, Parked in the Place Carrière, Neufchâteau, W. J. Duncan, May 18, 1918, pencil-and-ink sketch (*Smithsonian Institution*)

B2

Barber Shop and First-Aid Station of the Red Cross at Essey, W. J. Duncan,
September 17, 1918, pencil sketch (*Smithsonian Institution*)

B3

Baldwin Locomotives Unloaded as Shipped on the Wharf at Brest, W. J. Duncan, July 26, 1918, pencil sketch (*Smithsonian Institution*)

B4

Cold Nights Coming On, W. J. Duncan, October 20, 1918, ink sketch (*Smithsonian Institution*)

A Battery of French 75's Shelling the Germans on the Ridge to the Left of Château-Thierry, W. J. Duncan, June, 1918, pencil sketch (*Smithsonian Institution*)

B6

Off Duty, H. T. Dunn, undated, oil *(Smithsonian Institution)*

C1

In the Front Line at Early Morning, H. T. Dunn, undated, oil (*Smithsonian Institution*)

C2

The Engineer, H. T. Dunn, August, 1918, watercolor (*Smithsonian Institution*)

C3

C4

The Machine Gunner, H. T. Dunn, August, 1918, charcoal and watercolor (*Smithsonian Institution*)

No Mans Land, H. T. Dunn, October, 1918, charcoal (*Smithsonian Institution*)

C5

The Harvest Moon, H. T. Dunn, August, 1918, pastel sketch (*Smithsonian Institution*)

C6

The Flare, H. T. Dunn, September, 1918, crayon (*Smithsonian Institution*)

The Hand Grenade, H. T. Dunn, August, 1918, pastel, charcoal (*Smithsonian Institution*)

C8

Tanks at Seichprey [*sic*], H. T. Dunn, September, 1918, watercolor (*Smithsonian Institution*)

C9

Prisoners and Wounded, H. T. Dunn, October, 1918, watercolor (*Smithsonian Institution*)

C10

Kamerad—The Sniper, H. T. Dunn, September, 1918, unknown medium (*Smithsonian Institution*)

C11

C12

The Boche Looter, H. T. Dunn, July, 1918, charcoal with oil (*Smithsonian Institution*)

Tanks Attacking Early Sept. 26th between Avocourt and Montfaucon, G. M. Harding, September, 1918, unknown medium (*Smithsonian Institution*)

D1

Vanquished by the Boche Plane, G. M. Harding, September 29, 1918, crayon and charcoal (*Smithsonian Institution*)

D2

Verdun Offensive: Wounded Working Back to Advanced Aid Station, G. M.
Harding, October, 1918, pencil sketch (*Smithsonian Institution*)

D3

First Aid Station with American Wounded Carried in by Boche Prisoners Early in Verdun Offensive, G. M. Harding, September 26, 1918, crayon and charcoal (*Smithsonian Institution*)

D4

American Gun Fire Early Morning Opening Verdun Offensive, G. M. Harding, October, 1918, sketch (*National Archives*)

D5

Verdun Offensive: American Troops Following Barrage, G. M. Harding, October, 1918, charcoal sketch (*National Archives*)

D6

In Pursuit of the Enemy: American Troops Entering Village during Advance across the Marne, G. M. Harding, July 24, 1918, pastel sketch (*Smithsonian Institution*)

D7

To the Victor Belong the Spoils, G. M. Harding, October, 1918, crayon (*Smithsonian Institution*)

Morning Mess, Beaumont-Toul Sector, G. M. Harding, May, 1918, charcoal
(*Smithsonian Institution*)

A Cold Breakfast on the March, W. Morgan, undated, charcoal (*Smithsonian Institution*)

American Artillery Relieved at Deumx after Days of Hard Fighting, W. Morgan, July 19, 1918, unknown medium (*Smithsonian Institution*)

E2

Dugouts of the 5th Marines in Bois de Belleau, W. Morgan, July, 1918, charcoal sketch (*Smithsonian Institution*)

E3

Supply Trains on the Paris-Metz Road during the Battle of Belleau Wood, June 6, 1918, W. Morgan, July, 1918, charcoal (*Smithsonian Institution*)

E4

The Morning Washup, Neufmaison, W. Morgan, May, 1918, charcoal (*Smithsonian Institution*)

E5

Machine Gun Outfit Moving Forward near Esnes during the Artillery Attack,
Sept. 26, W. Morgan, September 26, 1918, charcoal (*National Archives*)

E6

Engineers Building Roads, W. Morgan, undated, pencil sketch (*National Archives*)

E7

Flirey, E. C. Peixotto, September, 1918, charcoal (*Smithsonian Institution*)

F1

Troops Leaving Esnes, E. C. Peixotto, October, 1918, unknown medium (*Smithsonian Institution*)

F2

No Man's Land, near Thiaucourt, E. C. Peixotto, January or February, 1919, charcoal (*Smithsonian Institution*)

F3

General Pershing Entering St. Mihiel, E. C. Peixotto, September, 1918, charcoal (*Smithsonian Institution*)

F4

German Shelters near Varennes, E. C. Peixotto, October, 1918, charcoal (*Smithsonian Institution*)

F5

Main Square, Montabaur, Headquarters of the 1st Division, E. C. Peixotto, January or February, 1919, charcoal (*National Archives*)

Boppard on the Rhine in the American Sector, E. C. Peixotto, January or February, 1919, charcoal and color (*Smithsonian Institution*)

F7

F8

First Americans Crossing the Rhine, E. C. Peixotto, January or February 1919, pencil sketch (*National Archives*)

Chaumont American Headquarters, J. A. Smith, February, 1919, pastel (*Smithsonian Institution*)

G1

A View of Neufchâteau, J. A. Smith, June, 1918, pastel (*Smithsonian Institution*)

G2

A Gateway to the Front, Rambucourt, J. A. Smith, undated, unknown medium (*Smithsonian Institution*)

G3

Flirey, J. A. Smith, September, 1918, charcoal (*Smithsonian Institution*)

G4

Pathway to Peace, J. A. Smith, undated, unknown medium (*Smithsonian Institution*)

G5

On the Edge of Rambucourt, J. A. Smith, undated, charcoal (*Smithsonian Institution*)

G6

Flying Field at Issoudun, J. A. Smith, February, 1919, unknown medium
(*Smithsonian Institution*)

A Tank Surprises and Cleans Up, H. E. Townsend, August, 1918, charcoal (*Smithsonian Institution*)

A Six-Ton Camouflaged Tank, H. E. Townsend, August, 1918, unknown
medium (*Smithsonian Institution*)

H2

The Light Tank in Action, H. E. Townsend, August, 1918, charcoal (*Smithsonian Institution*)

H3

The Alert Nieuports, H. E. Townsend, August, 1918, charcoal (*Smithsonian Institution*)

H4

A Forced Landing near Neufchâteau, H. E. Townsend, June, 1918, charcoal
(*Smithsonian Institution*)

H5

On the Gas Alert, H. E. Townsend, May, 1919, charcoal (*Smithsonian Institution*)

H6

Soldiers of the Telephone, H. E. Townsend, October, 1918, charcoal (*Smithsonian Institution*)

H7

Helping a Wounded Ally, H. E. Townsend, October, 1918, charcoal (*Smithsonian Institution*)

H8

Infantryman, H. E. Townsend, October, 1918, charcoal (*Smithsonian Institution*)

H9

Our Troops Entering Coblenz, H. E. Townsend, May, 1919, charcoal (*Smithsonian Institution*)

H10

Notes

Preface

1. J. André Smith, *In France with the American Expeditionary Forces* (New York: Arthur H. Hahlo and Co., 1919), from the foreword, n.p.
2. Adeline Adams, "Ernest Peixotto's War Landscapes," *American Magazine of Art* 12, no. 6 (June, 1921): 191.

Chapter 1

1. Aimée Crane, ed., *Marines at War* (New York: Hyperion Press, 1943), p. 7.
2. *American Battle Painting, 1776–1918* (Washington, D.C.: National Gallery of Art, [1944]), p. 5.
3. Quotations in Maria Tippett, *Art at the Service of War: Canada, Art, and the Great War* (Toronto: University of Toronto Press, 1984), pp. 57–58.
4. Denis Thomas, ed. and comp., *Arms and the Artist* (New York: Dutton, 1977), from the foreword, n.p.
5. Marian R. McNaughton, "The Army Art Program," in John E. Jessup, Jr., and Robert W. Coakley, eds., *A Guide to the Study and Use of Military History* (Washington, D.C.: Center for Military History, 1979), p. 319. For a summary treatment of U.S. military and naval art through history, with numerous examples of the pictures, see Library of Congress, *An Album of American Battle Art, 1755–1918* (Washington, D.C.: GPO, 1947); and the useful study by Roy Meredith, *The American Wars: A Pictorial History from Quebec to Korea, 1755–1953* (Cleveland: World Publishing, 1955).
6. Theodore Sizer, *The Works of Colonel John Trumbull*, rev. ed. (New Haven: Yale University Press, 1967).
7. There is a useful discussion of how artists treated the Mexican War in Robert Walker Johannsen, *To the Halls of the Montezumas: The Mexican War in the American Imagination* (New York: Oxford University Press, 1985), pp. 225–30.
8. For the Civil War and its art see especially Philip van Doren Stern, *They Were There: The Civil War in Action as Seen by Its Combat Artists* (New York: Crown Publishers, 1959); and Hermann Warner Williams, Jr., *The Civil War: The Artists' Record* (Washington, D.C.: Corcoran Gallery of Art, 1961).
9. For Remington in the West, see Douglas C. Jones, "Remington Reports from the Bad-

lands: The Artist as War Correspondent," *Journalism Quarterly* 47, no. 4 (Winter, 1970): 702–10. For Davis, see Edgar McPherson Howell, "Theodore R. Davis: Special Artist in the Indian Wars," *Montana* 15, no. 2 (Apr., 1965): 2–23.

10. Frank Freidel, *The Splendid Little War* (New York: Bramhall House, 1958), p. 308.

11. Albert Eugene Gallatin, *Art and the Great War* (New York: Dutton, 1919), p. 22.

12. Adams, "Ernest Peixotto's War Landscapes," pp. 193–94.

13. André Ducasse, Jacques Meyer, and Gabriel Perreux, *Vie et mort des français: 1914–1918* (Paris: Hachette, 1962), pp. 510–11. Also on camouflage, see Elizabeth Louise Kahn, *The Neglected Majority: "Les camoufleurs," Art History, and World War I* (Lanham, Md.: University Press of America, 1984).

14. On war cartoons, see Broadman Robinson, *Cartoons on the War* (New York: Dutton, 1915); H. Pearl Adam, ed. *International Cartoons of the War* (New York: Dutton, n.d.); J. Murray Allison, comp., *Raemaekers' Cartoon History of the War* (New York: Century, 1918); and George J. Hecht, ed., *The War in Cartoons* (New York: Garland, 1971).

15. For the British war art efforts, see the excellent study by Meirion Harries and Susie Harries, *The War Artists: British Official War Art of the Twentieth Century* (London: Michael Joseph in Association with the Imperial War Museum and the Tate Gallery, 1983).

16. Ibid., p. 2.

17. Gallatin, *Art and the Great War*, pp. 133, 135.

18. Ibid., p. 143.

19. Kimberly Keefer, "The Art of Henry Farré," *American History Illustrated* 17, no. 5 (Sept., 1982): 30–31.

20. Gallatin, *Art and the Great War*, pp. 225–27.

21. For poster art, see Martin Hardie and Arthur K. Sabin, eds., *War Posters Issued by Belligerent and Neutral Nations, 1914–1919* (London: A. and C. Black, 1920); and Maurice Richards, *Posters of the First World War* (New York: Walker and Co., 1968).

22. Russell Lynes, *The Lively Audience: A Social History of the Visual and Performing Arts in America, 1890–1950* (New York: Harper and Row, 1985), p. 322; Stephen Vaughn, *Holding Fast the Inner Lines: Democracy, Nationalism, and the Committee on Public Information* (Chapel Hill: University of North Carolina Press, 1980), p. 149. For an account of Gibson's life, see Fairfax Downey, *Portrait of an Era as Drawn by C. D. Gibson* (New York: Charles Scribner's Sons, 1936).

23. Committee on Public Information, *Complete Report of the Chairman of the Committee on Public Information* (Washington, D.C.: GPO, 1920), p. 40; George Creel, *How We Advertised America* (New York: Harper and Brothers, 1920), pp. 133–34.

24. Specifics are in Committee on Public Information, *Complete Report*, pp. 40–43.

25. Gallatin, *Art and the Great War*, p. 39; Creel, *How We Advertised America*, p. 138.

26. See examples of Christy's work in Susan E. Meyer, "Howard Chandler Christy," *American Artist* 42, no. 430 (May, 1978): 42–47, 98–101.

27. Gallatin, *Art and the Great War*, p. 43. For Pennell's work, see *Joseph Pennell's Pictures of War Work in America* (Philadelphia: Lippincott, 1918).

28. Gallatin, *Art and the Great War*, pp. 49–51.

29. J. R. Cornelius, "The Value of Landscape Targets: Their Use in Musketry," *Scribner's*

Magazine 64, no. 4 (Oct., 1918): 433–40; "Landscape Targets," *American Magazine of Art* 10, no. 2 (Dec., 1918): 47–48.

30. Grace S. Harper, "New Faces for Mutilated Soldiers," *Red Cross Magazine* 13, no. 11 (Nov., 1918): 44–45.

31. Gallatin, *Art and the Great War,* p. 48.

32. Ibid., p. 56; "A Notable Series of Mural Paintings Executed for the Victory Celebration, New York," *American Magazine of Art* 10, no. 12 (Oct., 1919): 475–78.

33. Gallatin, *War and the Great War,* p. 53.

34. Ibid., pp. 41–42. Chase's considerable activity is discussed, and his work displayed, in his two books: *Soldiers All* (New York: George H. Doran, 1929) and *Speaking of Heroes* (Wauwatosa, Wis.: Rudolf Binzel and Marion Lemonds, 1972). For Samuel Johnson Woolf, see his memoirs, *Here Am I* (New York: Random House, 1941).

35. *American Battle Painting, 1776–1918,* pp. 11–12.

Chapter 2

1. Much of the account regarding the selection of the artists is from Capt. J. André Smith, report to Maj. A. L. James, Jr., chief of G-2D, Oct. 21, 1918, in Folder 4, Drawer 3, Case 70, Entry 224, Record Group 120, National Archives, Washington, D.C. (Since the archival documents used in this study are all from Drawer 3, Case 70, Entry 224, only the individual folder numbers will be referred to in subsequent citations from this record group.)

2. Gallatin, *Art and the Great War,* p. 39; Creel, *How We Advertised America,* pp. 117–19.

3. This committee included, in addition to Gibson, Herbert Adams, a sculptor; Joseph Pennell, an artist-illustrator; Cass Gilbert, an architect; Edwin H. Blashfield, past president of the Society of American Artists; Oliver D. Grover, past president of the Society of Western Artists; Arthur T. Mathews, former director of the California School of Design; Edmund C. Tarbell, president of the Guild of Boston Artists; and Francis C. Jones, representative of the American Water Color Society and Society of Mural Painters.

4. There is also a discussion of the artists' selection in Robert F. Karolevitz, *Where Your Heart Is: The Story of Harvey Dunn, Artist* (Aberdeen, S.Dak.: North Plains Press, 1970), pp. 51–52.

5. Brief biographical sketch of Aylward on Frame 601 (hereafter cited as Aylward, Frame 601), Roll N76 of "Prints Division, New York Public Library" collection, Archives of American Art, National Portrait Gallery (hereafter AAA/NPG), Washington, D.C.

6. For the remarkable Pyle, see Rowland Elzea, *Howard Pyle* (New York: Peacock Press, 1975); Henry Clarence Pitz, *Howard Pyle* (New York: Clarkson N. Potter, 1975); and Susan E. Meyer, *America's Great Illustrators* (New York: Harry N. Abrams, 1978), pp. 43–56 and plates section.

7. Some of Aylward's articles, which appeared in *Scribner's Magazine* and were illustrated with his own drawings, included: "How They Rammed the Derelict," 43, no. 4 (Apr., 1908): 385–93; "The Old Man-of-War's Man: English Naval Life in the Eighteenth Century," 60, no. 1 (Jan., 1914): 31–45; and "The Clipper-Ship and Her Seamen," 61, no. 4 (Apr., 1917): 387–403.

8. Biographical sketch of Aylward by Florence S. Berryman in Aylward File, library of the Pennsylvania Academy of the Fine Arts, Philadelphia, 1926 (hereafter cited as Berry-

man, Aylward Biography). See also Walt Reed, comp. and ed., *The Illustrator in America, 1900–1960's* (New York: Reinhold Publishing, 1966), p. 45.

9. "The Sea Voyage of a Dry-Dock," *Scribner's Magazine* 41, no. 5 (May, 1907): 513–36. Aylward's experiences were further drawn upon in illustrating another article in the same issue by Charles M. Pepper, "The West in the Orient . . . The Westward Tide of Commerce through Suez," pp. 434–49.

10. Aylward wrote and illustrated other articles based on his encounter with the Orient. These included: "The Water-Life around Singapore," *Harper's Monthly Magazine* 120 (Dec., 1909): 106–14; and "Hong-Kong," *Harper's Monthly Magazine* 121 (Aug., 1910): 392–403. See also Berryman, Aylward Biography.

11. Reed, *Illustrator in America*, p. 45; Berryman, Aylward Biography.

12. Officer's Qualification Report for Capt. William James Aylward, Feb. 25, 1919; memorandum, G-2D, to Captain Aylward, May 10, 1918; Captain Aylward, monthly report for May, 1918, to Chief, G-2D, June 1, 1918, all in Folder 9.

13. Anice Page Cooper, *About Artists* (Garden City, N.Y.: Doubleday, Page, 1926), n.p.

14. Ibid.

15. Reed, *Illustrator in America*, p. 51.

16. Quoted in Cooper, *About Artists*, n.p.

17. Ibid.

18. Robert F. Karolevitz, *The Prairie Is My Garden: The Story of Harvey Dunn* (Aberdeen, S.Dak.: North Plains Press, 1969), and *Where Your Heart Is*. There is additional information on Dunn's family connectons in Judith Miner Hine Luedemann, *The Ancestry of Harvey Dunn* (Chester, Conn.: Pequot Press, 1973); John Jellico, "Harvey Dunn, 1884–1952," *Artists of the Rockies and the Golden West* 8, no. 4 (Fall, 1981): 88–96; and Edgar M. Howell, "An Artist Goes To War: Harvey Dunn and the A.E.F. War Art Program," *Smithsonian Journal of History* 2 (Winter, 1967–68): 45–56.

    The archives of the South Dakota Memorial Art Center, on the campus of South Dakota State University, at Brookings, possesses a large collection of Dunn materials and memorabilia. In addition, the center owns seventy-four Dunn paintings and two drawings. Only one of the latter, *Pontoon Crossing*, is of the World War I era, it being a sketch done in the field and not submitted as part of Dunn's official production.

19. Henry Clarence Pitz, "Four Disciples of Howard Pyle," *American Artist* 33, no. 1 (Jan., 1969): 38–43; Harvey T. Dunn, Frank E. Schoonover, et al., *The Howard Pyle Brandywine Edition, 1853–1933* (New York: Scribner's, 1933); Richard McLanathan, *The Brandywine Heritage* (Greenwich: New York Graphic Society, 1971); and Henry Clarence Pitz, *The Brandywine Tradition* (Boston: Houghton Mifflin, 1969), and also by Pitz, *200 Years of American Illustration* (New York: Random House, 1977).

20. See, for example, Ernest William Hornung, *Dead Men Tell No Tales* (New York: Charles Scribner's Sons, 1906), the first book that Dunn illustrated; Rex Ellingwood Beach, *The Silver Horde* (New York: Harper and Brothers, 1909); and Jack London, *John Barleycorn* (New York: Grosset and Dunlap, 1913).

21. James J. Fahey, *Pacific War Diary, 1942–1945* (New York: Avon Books, 1963), pp. 127–28.

22. Reed, *Illustrator in America*, pp. 25, 59.

23. George Harding, "Drawing the War," *American Magazine of Art* 32, no. 10 (Oct., 1939): 569.

24. George Harding, "When Our Ship Went Down: An Adventure with the Sealing Fleet off Newfoundland," *Harper's Monthly Magazine* 118 (Apr., 1909): 659–72; "Wreckers of the Florida Keys," *Harper's Monthly Magazine* 123 (July, 1911): 275–85.

25. George Harding, "The Menace of Cape Race," *Harper's Monthly Magazine* 124 (Apr., 1912): 674–84.

26. Harding, "Drawing the War," p. 570.

27. Dorothy Grafly, "George Harding Show Spans Half Century," *Philadelphia, Pa., Bulletin,* Nov. 3, 1957.

28. George Harding, "Coaling-Ports of the World," *Harper's Monthly Magazine* 133 (June, 1916): 27–37. Although rather brief, this article describes and illustrates some of the world's more exotic ports, e.g., Port Said, Singapore, Gibraltar, Sydney, and Cape Town, and their hinterlands. See also illustrations in Norman Duncan, *Australian Byways* (New York: Harper and Brothers, 1915).

29. For Harding's early murals, see Eva Nagel Wolf, "Murals by Harding," *International Studio* 62, no. 245 (July, 1917): xvi–xviii, which discusses his decorations in the Hotel Traymore in Atlantic City. His murals there revealed the influences of his travels in the Orient. Information on family and career in Chief of Engineers, War Department, Washington, D.C., memorandum to Commanding General, Port of Embarkation, Hoboken, N.J., undated, but ca. Apr., 1918, Folder 6. This memorandum was for the purpose of assisting in properly assigning Harding.

30. Harding, "Drawing the War," pp. 570–72. This article contains a brief diary account of Harding's voyage over.

31. "Wallace Morgan," *Etchings* (June, 1939): n.p.

32. Reed, *Illustrator in America*, p. 62. Morgan's first published work, however, consisted of a set of five drawings illustrating the Easter gospel for the *Churchman*. See discussion in "Wallace Morgan," *Etchings*, n.p.

33. Louis H. Frohman, "Wallace Morgan, Illustrator," *International Studio* 78, no. 320 (Jan., 1924): 356.

34. Anonymous, "The Wallace Morgan Story," p. 6, typescript in "Morgan, Wallace (1873–1948)" folder, library of the Society of Illustrators, New York City; Reed, *Illustrator in America*, p. 62.

35. Anon., "The Wallace Morgan Story," p. 8.

36. Quoted in ibid., pp. 2, 7. See also Carolyn Wells, *Fluffy Ruffles: Drawings by Wallace Morgan, Verses by Carolyn Wells* (New York: D. Appleton, 1907).

37. Julian Leonard Street, *Abroad at Home: American Ramblings, Observations, and Adventures of Julian Street* [by Julian Street, with pictorial sidelights by Wallace Morgan] (New York: Century, 1914). See also the work, Julian Leonard Street, *Welcome to Our City* [with illustrations by James Montgomery Flagg and Wallace Morgan] (New York: John Lane, [1913]), on New York City.

38. There is a short biography of Peixotto in a series on California artists written under the auspices of the 1930s Works Progress Administration. See vol. IX, pp. 30–62, on Roll NDA/CAL 1, "California Art Research" collection, AAA/NPG.

39. Ernest Clifford Peixotto, *Through the French Provinces* (New York: Charles Scribner's

Sons, 1909), pp. v, 16–17. In 1893, Peixotto also exhibited works at the World's Columbian Exposition in Chicago, receiving an honorable mention.

40. Ibid., pp. 52–53; Winston Spencer Churchill, *The World Crisis, 1911–1918*, (rpt., London: Landsborough Publications, 1960), p. 111.

41. All published by Charles Scribner's Sons of New York, Peixotto's travel books included *By Italian Seas* (1906), *Romantic California* (1910), *Pacific Shores from Panama* (1913), *Our Hispanic Southwest* (1916), and *A Revolutionary Pilgrimage* (1917). Among his illustrated travel articles are "Lisbon and Cintra," *Scribner's Magazine* 58, no. 2 (Aug., 1915): 191–204, and "Portugal's Battle Abbeys and Coimbra," *Scribner's Magazine* 58, no. 4 (Oct., 1915): 479–93.

42. Among the books Peixotto illustrated were Theodore Roosevelt, *Life of Cromwell* (1900); Henry Cabot Lodge's two-volume study, *The Story of the Revolution* (1898); Charles Hemstreet, *Nooks and Corners of Old New York* (1899), all published by Scribner's, and Agnes Repplier, *Philadelphia: The Place and the People* (New York: Macmillan, 1898).

43. Ernest Clifford Peixotto, *The American Front* (New York: Charles Scribner's Sons, 1919), p. xiv. This book is Peixotto's memoir of his experiences in World War I, including his service as official artist.

44. Exhibition catalog, *The European Etchings of J. André Smith (1880–1959)*, for a retrospective at the June 1 Gallery, Bethlehem, Connecticut, Sept. 18 to Oct. 10, 1976. Copy in folder, "Smith, J. André, 1880–1959" in vertical files of the National Portrait Gallery's library, Washington, D.C.

45. For biographical sketches of Smith, see undated mimeographed fact sheet, "André Smith, 1880–1959," in André Smith file, Maitland Public Library, Maitland, Florida (cited hereafter as "André Smith, 1880–1959," MPL), and notes by Thomas W. Leavitt, in exhibition catalog for a retrospective of Smith's art at the Andrew Dickson White Museum of Art, Cornell University in 1968 (Winston-Salem, N.C.: Hunter Publishing, 1969) (cited hereafter as Leavitt, Exhibition Catalog).

46. Smith's early development as an etcher is discussed in a booklet by Lena M. McCauley, *J. André Smith: Painter-Etcher* (Chicago: Roullier's Art Rooms, 1910), pp. 3–16 (found in frames 367–76, Roll N108, "Prints Division, NYPL" collection, AAA/NPG). See also frames 381–86, and 404–409, for catalogs announcing showings of Smith's work at the galleries of the Arthur H. Hahlo Company (Smith's New York dealer) for Feb., 1914, and Feb., 1915 (Roullier's Art Galleries served as his Chicago agent). Smith was soon being compared with John Taylor Arms, Louis C. Rosenberg, and Samuel Chamberlain. So many artists were doing architectural etchings in the early twentieth century, that Smith must have reached high standards in order to attract any attention at all, much less favorable comparisons. Another influential critic who warmly praised Smith's accomplishments was J. Nilsen Laurvik. See his article, "J. André Smith," *Print-Collectors Quarterly* 4, no. 2 (Apr., 1914): 167–82. This was reprinted as a booklet by Arthur H. Hahlo (copy in frames 387–402).

47. Leavitt, Exhibition Catalog.

48. "André Smith, 1880–1959," MPL, p. 2. There is a critique of Smith's developing career as etcher in Helen Wright, "J. André Smith—Etcher," *American Magazine of Art* 12 (Oct., 1918): 485–89. See also "Etchings by J. André Smith," *Country Life* 33, no. 3

(Jan., 1918): 33–35. These examples were from an exhibit that had recently been held at the Hahlo Galleries.

49. J. André Smith, "Notes on Camouflage," *Architectural Record* 42 (July–Dec., 1917): 469.

50. Officer's Qualification Report on Capt. J. André Smith, Feb. 25, 1919, and Lt. Col. Aristides Moreno, Army Chief of Staff, G-2, memorandum to Commanding Officer, Officers' Casual Camp, Angers, France, Feb. 7, 1919, both in Folder 4.

51. There are biographical sketches in articles in the *New Canaan* [Conn.] *Advertiser,* Aug. 23, 1934; the *Bridgeport* [Conn.] *Sunday Post,* Oct. 9, 1938; and the *Norwalk* [Conn.] *Hour,* July 30, 1941.

52. In 1910, the City Art Museum of St. Louis featured some of Townsend's illustrations, together with work of the illustrators John Scott Williams, Charles S. Chapman, Howard McCormick, and John Rutherford Boyd. See exhibition catalog published by the museum: *A Collection of Works by Five American Illustrators.*

53. GHQ, AEF, Officer's Qualification Report for Capt. Harry E. Townsend, Feb. 25, 1919, Folder 2.

Chapter 3

1. Peixotto, *American Front,* p. xiv; Tulla Dunn quoted in Karolevitz, *Where Your Heart Is,* pp. 52–53.

2. Peixotto, *American Front,* pp. 3–23. Wallace Morgan was also on board this ship with Peixotto. Morgan, in a lengthy letter to his sister, recounted some of the details of his trip to France. His experiences were similar to those of Harding and Peixotto, both of whom left accounts of their voyages over. He too was amazed that he had to serve as officer of the day without any understanding of his duties. See his letter as quoted in anon., "Wallace Morgan Story," pp. 8–11.

3. Harding, "Drawing the War," p. 571.

4. Karolevitz, *Where Your Heart Is,* p. 53.

5. Peixotto, *American Front,* p. 14.

6. Ibid., pp. 16–17, 20–21.

7. William Henry Holaday III, "Harvey Dunn: Pioneer Painter of the Middle Border" (Ph.D. diss., Ohio State University, 1970), pp. 25–26.

8. Smith, Morgan and Peixotto set out to locate a base of operations for the artists. They rented a pavilion at 16 Rue Neuve in Neufchâteau. See the monthly reports to Chief, G-2D, for Apr., 1918, from Capt. Wallace Morgan, Folder 5; Capt. J. André Smith, Folder 4; and Capt. Ernest Peixotto, Folder 3; and GHQ, AEF, special orders No. 107, Apr. 17, 1918, to Captains Smith, Morgan, and Peixotto, Folder 3. For details of the conditions at Neufchâteau, see Emmet Crozier, *American Reporters on the Western Front, 1914–1918* (New York: Oxford University Press, 1959).

9. Peixotto, *American Front,* p. 23.

10. Ibid., p. 22; Chief, G-2D (Lt. Col. Walter C. Sweeney), memorandum, to the captains named, on the subject of their official duties, Apr. 30, 1918, Folder 3.

11. This memorandum, in Folder 10, was signed by Lt. Col. E. R. W. McCabe, then chief, G-2D.

12. Capt. J. André Smith to Colonel Steese, Aug. 14, 1918, in Folder, "Dunn reference. Ketcham, *et al.*; AEF 1918 May 2, *et al.*," in File, "Dunn: References," in South Da-

kota Memorial Art Center, Brookings, S.Dak. (hereafter cited as Folder, "Dunn reference," SDMAC).

13. The artists purchased their materials in Paris, usually sending one or more of the group there for that purpose. See monthly reports to Chief, G-2D, for Apr., 1918, from Capt. Ernest Peixotto, Folder 3; and Capt. J. André Smith, Folder 4; and Capt. Ernest Peixotto, memorandum to Chief, G-2D, June 15, 1918, Folder 3. The latter notes the receipt of a shipment of artists' supplies from Paris and requests that the vendor be paid.

14. Smith to Steese, Aug. 14, 1918, in Folder, "Dunn reference," SDMAC.

15. Peixotto, *American Front*, p. 23.

16. There is a discussion of Morgan's methods and some sketches from his wartime sketchbook in Ernest W. Watson, *Forty Illustrators and How They Work* (New York: Watson-Guptill Publications, 1946), pp. 204–10.

17. Capt. Wallace Morgan, monthly reports for May and June, 1918, to Chief, G-2D, both in Folder 5. Interestingly, once while sketching near Verdun, Morgan and Duncan encountered a car full of French officers who, seeing them at work, stopped and asked who the men were and what their mission was. The French officers "viewed their work enthusiastically, complimented them, thanked them and then drove away." Shortly thereafter they were confronted by an American officer, who, when being informed of their identity, exclaimed: "My God as if we didn't have enough trouble! They send us artists!" (anon., "Wallace Morgan Story," p. 13).

18. Capt. Wallace Morgan, monthly report for Aug., 1918, to Chief, G-2D; lists of pictures by Capt. Wallace Morgan, undated, and another for Oct., 1918, both in Folder 5.

19. Capt. Wallace Morgan, monthly reports for June and July, 1918, to Chief, G-2D; GHQ, AEF, memorandum to Capt. Wallace Morgan, June 10, 1918, all in Folder 5. Morgan had earlier drawn four illustrations for *Stars and Stripes*.

20. Capt. Harry E. Townsend, monthly reports for May and Aug., 1918, to Chief, G-2D, Folder 2.

21. Capt. Harry E. Townsend, monthly reports for June through Nov., 1918, to Chief, G-2D, all in Folder 2.

22. GHQ, AEF, special orders No. 190, paragraph 78, to Capt. W. J. Duncan, July 9, 1918; Capt. W. J. Duncan, monthly report for July, 1918, to Chief, G-2D, both in Folder 8.

23. Peixotto, *American Front*, pp. 28, 34–37.

24. Capt. Ernest Peixotto, monthly report for May, 1918, to Chief, G-2D, Folder 3; Peixotto, *American Front*, pp. 43–64.

25. Capt. Ernest Peixotto, monthly report for June, 1918, to Chief, G-2D, Folder 3; Peixotto, *American Front*, pp. 67–100.

26. Peixotto, *American Front*, pp. 111–12.

27. GHQ, AEF, special orders No. 177, paragraph 90, to Captains Peixotto and Smith, June 26, 1918; Capt. Ernest Peixotto, monthly reports for July and Aug., 1918, to Chief, G-2D; and Army Chief of Staff, G-2, GHQ, AEF, travel orders, to Capt. Ernest Peixotto, Aug. 24, 1918, all in Folder 3.

28. Capt. Ernest Peixotto, monthly report for Sept., 1918, to Chief, G-2D, Folder 3.

29. Peixotto, *American Front*, pp. 127, 134–44.

30. Capt. Ernest Peixotto, monthly report for Sept., 1918, to Chief, G-2D, Folder 3.

31. Peixotto, *American Front,* pp. 157, 163, 176; Capt. Ernest Peixotto, monthly report for Oct., 1918, to Chief, G-2D, Folder 3.

32. Chief, G-2D, letter and memorandum to Capt. Ernest Peixotto, Oct. 25, 1918, both in Folder 3.

33. Peixotto, *American Front,* pp. 179–80.

34. Ibid., pp. 181–84.

35. Memoranda, from Lt. Col. W. S. Sweeney, Chief, G-2D, to Capt. J. André Smith, Apr. 19, 1918; from Capt. J. André Smith to Chief, G-2D, May 4, 1918, both in Folder 4. Smith's first drawings featured the villages of Badonviller and Pexonne (Capt. J. André Smith, monthly report for Apr., 1918, to Chief, G-2D, Folder 4).

36. Capt. J. André Smith, memorandum to Lt. Col. E. R. W. McCabe, July 28, 1918, Folder 4.

37. Assistant Press Officer, G-2D, memorandum to Capt. George M. Harding, May 15, 1918, Folder 6 (2d Lt. Joe T. Marshall, a cavalry officer, was the Assistant Press Officer, G-2D, at this time.); Capt. George M. Harding, monthly report for June, 1918, to Chief, G-2D, Folder 6. Rather uncharacteristic for an official report, Harding wanted, though, to "express my appreciation of the attitude of Section G-2D toward the work I am undertaking." The Chief, G-2D, changed several times in the summer of 1918. Lt. Col. W. C. Sweeney was the first chief; he was soon replaced by Lt. Col. E. R. W. McCabe; by early Aug., 1918, Maj. A. L. James, Jr., had taken over. For a considerable time, the efficient, capable assistant chief of G-2D was Capt. Mark S. Watson, a field artillery officer. Watson (promoted to major) later departed Chaumont for Paris, where he became officer-in-charge of *Stars and Stripes,* remaining until that paper terminated its career in June, 1919.

38. Capt. George M. Harding, monthly report for July, 1918, to Chief, G-2D, Folder 6.

39. Harding, "Drawing the War," pp. 572–73.

40. George Harding, "The American Artist at the Front," *American Magazine of Art* 10, no. 12 (Oct., 1919): 451.

41. Ibid., pp. 452–54; Maj. Kendall Banning, Office of the Chief of Staff, Washington, D.C., to Capt. George M. Harding, Oct. 25, 1918, Folder 6.

42. Harding, "The American Artist at the Front," p. 456.

43. Harding, "Drawing the War," p. 606.

44. Capt. George M. Harding, monthly reports for Aug. and Sept., 1918, to Chief, G-2D, Folder 6.

45. Capt. George M. Harding, monthly reports for Oct. and Nov., 1918, to Chief, G-2D, Folder 6.

46. Karolevitz, *Where Your Heart Is,* p. 53. This biography contains illustrations of Dunn's sketch box.

47. Karolevitz, *Where Your Heart Is,* p. 55. The South Dakota Memorial Art Center now owns Dunn's harmonica.

48. Capt. Harvey Dunn, monthly report for Aug., 1918, to Chief, G-2D, Folder 7.

49. Howell, "An Artist Goes to War," pp. 49–51.

50. Capt. Harvey Dunn, monthly report for Sept., 1918, to Chief, G-2D, Folder 7.

51. Capt. Harvey Dunn, monthly reports for Oct. and Nov., 1918, to Chief, G-2D, Folder 7.

52. War Department, cablegram, No. 1711-R, paragraph 25, to Gen. John J. Pershing, July 13, 1918, Folder 10.

53. Gen. John J. Pershing, courier cablegram No. 1480-S, paragraph 6-A, to War Department, July 18, 1918, Folder 10. The text of this cablegram was obviously drafted by Colonel Nolan and his staff at G-2. See Col. D. E. Nolan, memorandum to Chief of Staff, AEF, July 17, 1918, Folder 10. Nolan stated that "it is believed that Washington's apparent dissatisfaction with the work of the official artists received in Washington . . . is justified by the facts then at their disposal." However, it was also his opinion "that with one or two exceptions the artists are doing reasonably good work and it would be unwise to make any changes at present, as it would simply mean a period of a month or two of developing new men for work as military artists." There is no indication of who the "one or two exceptions" were.

54. Maj. Kendall Banning to Capt. J. André Smith, Aug. 13, 1918, Folder 10.

55. War Department, courier cablegram No. 13, paragraph 1, to Pershing, Aug. 26, 1918, Folder 10. Banning elaborated upon his views in a letter to Morgan in late September. "To be frank we do not know what to do with the little architectural renderings that we receive. They convey no information of military value and the magazines do not want them. The vast percentage of the pictures received to date show either ruined buildings or French landscape or village scenes. We are having these drawings put carefully away in the files in the hope that they may some day be of some value to somebody, although at the present time there seems to be no market for them." He wanted Morgan to impress upon his colleagues the need for *"action pictures* and *human interest pictures."* He was pleased to note encouraging signs in some of the pictures, especially in those of Harding, Townsend, and in Morgan. Banning had also talked with Gibson, who was particularly sensitive over the quantity and quality of the pictures that had been received. He felt that the disappointment expressed by the General Staff was "in a measure a reflection upon him and the men who recommended you all for appointment." Yet Banning was sympathetic to the artists' situation, observing that the "fault lies very largely in the fact that you were sent overseas without an adequate idea of your functions and without proper equipment and instructions. The thing was done in a haphazard way and much valuable time was lost." He did not despair, though: "I personally have faith that most of you Official Artists will make good; I have special confidence in you and in 4 others; perhaps it would be wise not to mention names at this time" (Major Banning to Captain Morgan, Sept. 23, 1918, in collection titled: "Portfolio of World War Sketches," Sanford Low Fund, 70.57.1-214 LIC, in the Sanford Low Memorial Collection of American Illustration, New Britain Museum of American Art, New Britain, Conn., hereafter cited as "Portfolio of World War Sketches," 70.57.1-214 LIC).

56. Pershing, draft of cablegram to the War Department, Sept. 19, 1918, Folder 10. This was no doubt soon dispatched, though on which date is not certain.

57. Maj. A. L. James, Jr., memorandum to all official artists, Sept. 19, 1918, Folder 10.

58. Capt. J. André Smith, report to Chief, G-2D, Oct. 21, 1918, Folder 4. See also Capt. Harry E. Townsend, memorandum to Chief, G-2D, Nov. 16, 1918, Folder 2, in which he also complained about many of the same things Smith presented in his report.

59. Maj. A. L. James, Jr., Chief of G-2D, memorandum to Brig. Gen. D. E. Nolan, Sept. 9, 1918, and Commander-in-Chief, AEF, memorandum to Adjutant General of the Army, Washington, D.C., undated but ca. early Sept., 1918, both in Folder 4.

60. Maj. Kendall Banning to Capt. J. André Smith, Sept. 30, 1918, Folder 4. Banning's change in tone may have been influenced by Smith's letter in mid-September in which he stated: "In regard to your criticism of our work I must confess that my position renders me powerless to reply to you as I would if the matter were a purely personal one." He noted that he had felt it necessary to bring Banning's complaints to the attention of his chief and added, "I presume that this matter will be taken up with you through the Intelligence Section at General Headquarters" (Capt. J. André Smith to Maj. Kendall Banning, undated but ca. mid-Sept., 1918, Folder 4).

    Certainly Harding had reason to be pleased with the reception of his work in Washington. As far as can be ascertained, only he received a letter from Banning warmly commending him. "Your pictures," Banning assured him, "have attracted favorable comment from every one who has seen them." The subjects that Harding had chosen "are good and indicate that you have an understanding of the character of the pictures which the War Department desires," he continued. This favorable response would make it probable that Harding's pictures, "though small in number, will receive a larger circulation than any of the pictures which have so far arrived" (Maj. Kendall Banning to Capt. George Harding, Oct. 25, 1918, Folder 6).

61. There is some confusion as to the total number of pictures selected by the magazines. Apparently the figure was forty. See memoranda, from Col. C. W. Weeks, Chief, Historical Branch, War Department to Capt. J. André Smith, Jan. 8, 1919, Folder 4; and Weeks to Chief of Engineers, Washington, D.C., Jan. 18, 1919, in Folder, "Dunn reference," SDMAC, which gives the total as thirty-nine. Of the drawings, *Century* selected eight; *Scribner's*, eight; *Leslie's Weekly*, five; *Farm and Fireside*, three; and *Collier's*, three. The selections ranged from fifteen works by Morgan down to Duncan's one. None of Dunn's works had yet arrived.

62. Maj. A. L. James, Jr., memorandum to Army Chief of Staff, G-2, Nov. 29, 1918, Folder 10.

63. Lt. Col. E. R. W. McCabe, to Col. Ulysses G. McAlexander, Aug. 6, 1918, Folder 4.

64. Assistant Chief, G-2D, memorandum to Chief, G-2D, June 1, 1918, Folder 3. At this time, Lt. Col. E. R. W. McCabe was the Assistant and Col. Walter C. Sweeney was Chief, G-2D. Peixotto stated that he made the report only at McCabe's request and out of "no personal animus."

65. Assistant Chief, G-2D, memorandum to Chief, G-2D, June 1, 1918, and four endorsements, Folder 3.

66. Capt. Mark S. Watson to Maj. Gen. William G. Haan, Sept. 20, 1918, Folder 3.

67. Memoranda, from Maj. A. L. James, Jr., to Brig. Gen. D. E. Nolan, Nov. 10, 1918; and from Brig. Gen. D. E. Nolan to Chief of Staff, AEF, Nov. 19, 1918, Folder 10.

68. Gen. John J. Pershing, draft of cable to War Department, Nov. 19, 1918; War Department, confidential cable No. 2243-R, paragraph 1, to Gen. John J. Pershing, Nov. 24, 1918, both in Folder 10.

Chapter 4

1. Captain Aylward, monthly reports to Chief, G-2D, for June through Dec., 1918, and memorandum to Chief, G-2D, Jan. 11, 1919, all in Folder 9. There are several documents in Folder 9 having to do with payment of utilities and the studio rent, which was 320 francs per month, paid in advance by the month. These matters were handled by the AEF's Paris office of Rents, Requisitions, and Claims.

2. Captain Aylward, memoranda to Chief, G-2D, Dec. 20 and 30, 1918, both in Folder 9.

3. GHQ, AEF, special orders no. 6, paragraph 41, to Captain Aylward, Jan. 6, 1919, Folder 9. Aylward was also provided with an open letter to all commanding officers of the Base Ports, AEF, introducing him, stating his business, and ordering them to "extend to Captain Aylward all available facilities to assist him in this duty" (see Brig. Gen. D. E. Nolan, Army Chief of Staff, G-2 [Intelligence], to the Commanding Officers, Base Ports, AEF, Jan. 6, 1919).

4. Captain Aylward, monthly reports for Jan. through Apr., 1919, and memorandum to Chief, G-2D, May 11, 1919, both in Folder 9.

5. Memoranda, from Captain Aylward to Chief, G-2D, May 11, 1919, to Capt. Donald L. Stone, May 11, 1919, to Major Stone, May 12 and 22, 1919; from Maj. Donald L. Stone to Captain Aylward, May 10 and 14, 1919, all in Folder 9. Stone, who had just been promoted to major, duly informed the commanding officer of the casual camp at St. Aignan that Captain Aylward had no military training or experience and "was commissioned solely to give his work as an official artist an army standing and, therefore, should not be put in charge of troops returning to the United States" (Maj. Donald L. Stone, memorandum to Commanding Officer, Officers' Casual Camp, St. Aignan, June 7, 1919, Folder 9).

6. Telegrams, from Captain Aylward to Maj. Donald L. Stone, June 7, 1919; from Brig. Gen. D. E. Nolan to Captain Aylward, June 7, 1919; from Captain Aylward to Chief, G-2D, June 9, 1919; and special orders no. 157, paragraph 103, to Captain Aylward, June 6, 1919, Folder 9. Stone attempted to obtain permission for Aylward to sail from Marseilles but the SOS authorities would not permit it. See Maj. Donald L. Stone, memorandum to commanding Officers' Casual Camp, St. Aignan, June 7, 1919, Folder 9.

7. Capt. W. J. Duncan, monthly report for Nov., 1918, to Chief, G-2D, Folder 8.

8. Capt. W. J. Duncan, combined monthly reports for Jan., Feb., and Mar., 1919, to Chief, G-2D, Folder 8.

9. Memoranda, from Brig. Gen. D. E. Nolan to Chief of Staff, AEF; from Maj. Donald E. Stone to Col. Aristides Moreno, Acting Secretary, G-2; draft of cablegram, from GHQ, AEF, to War Department, all May 31, 1919, all in Folder 8; GHQ, AEF, special orders no. 165, paragraph 50, to Capt. Walter J. Duncan, June 14, 1919, Folder 8. Unlike some of the other artists, Duncan skipped St. Aignan, reporting directly to the commanding general, Base Section No. 5, at Brest for embarkation.

10. Capt. Harvey Dunn, memorandum to Chief, G-2D, Dec. 19, 1918, Folder 7.

11. G-2, GHQ, AEF, memorandum to Commanding General SOS, Jan. 15, 1919; telegrams, from Capt. Harvey Dunn to Chief, G-2D, and from Capt. Donald L. Stone to Capt. Harvey Dunn, both Jan. 23, 1919, all in Folder 7.

12. Karolevitz, *Where Your Heart Is*, pp. 67–71. See Harvey Dunn to Col. C. W. Weeks, New York City, Apr. 15, 1919, in which Dunn requested an immediate discharge if he could not be permitted to continue on active duty to complete his artwork. This was almost immediately accepted by the army. See also Weeks's reply, dated Apr. 19, 1919, both in Folder, "Dunn reference," SDMAC.

13. Ernest W. Watson, "Harvey Dunn: Milestone in the Tradition of American Illustra-

tion," *American Artist* 6, no. 6 (June, 1942): 16; Watson, *Forty Illustrators and How They Work*, pp. 116–20.

14. Pitz, "Four Disciples of Howard Pyle," pp. 42–43. There is considerable information on and by Dunn's students in the files "Dunn: References" and "Dunn: Biographical," SDMAC.

15. Karolevitz, *Where Your Heart Is*, p. 88; Jellico, "Harvey Dunn," p. 96; Watson, "Harvey Dunn," p. 16; Saul Tepper, "Harvey Dunn: The Man, the Legend, the School of Painting," notes in exhibition catalog for showing held by the Society of Illustrators, New York City, June 1–23, 1983. Tepper was a former Dunn student and was elected to the Society of Illustrators' Hall of Fame in 1980.

16. Karolevitz, *Where Your Heart Is*, p. 67, and *The Prairie Is My Garden*, p. 61.

17. Quoted in Karolevitz, *Where Your Heart Is*, p. 94.

18. Details of this exhibition and its consequences are discussed in Aubrey Sherwood, *Harvey Dunn: Master Mason* (De Smet, S.Dak.: South Dakota Lodge of Masonic Research, 1964); Karolevitz, *Where Your Heart Is*, p. 129.

19. In 1968, the South Dakota State University Educational Media Department produced a twenty-four-minute color film, scripted by John D. Wheeler, on Dunn's life and career, with emphasis on his Dakota and frontier paintings, though some discussion of his World War I art is included.

20. Representative of this literature is: Edgar McPherson Howell, "Harvey Dunn: Searching Artist of the West," *Montana* 16, no. 1 (Jan., 1966): 41–56; Edgar McPherson Howell, *Harvey Dunn: Painter of Pioneers* (Helena: Montana Historical Society, 1967); and "'The Prairie Is My Garden': Nature Scenes by Harvey Thomas Dunn," *American History Illustrated* 15, no. 1 (Apr., 1980): 25–29.

21. These exhibitions have included: fifty-two paintings and drawings at the Brandywine River Museum, Chadds Ford, Pa., Sept. 7 to Nov. 24, 1974, the first major show of Dunn's work on the East Coast; and also at the Brandywine River Museum, June 4 to Sept. 26, 1976, an exhibition that included eight of Dunn's World War I pictures and selections from the work of the other seven official artists; "Battle Art: American Expeditionary Forces, 1918," at the Museum of History and Technology, Smithsonian Institution, Washington, D.C., Apr. 17 to June 27, 1967; and Society of Illustrators exhibition, "The Harvey Dunn School," New York City, June 1 to June 23, 1983.

22. Capt. George M. Harding, memorandum to Chief, G-2D, Dec. 8, 1918, and monthly reports for Nov. and Dec., 1918, to Chief, G-2D, all in Folder 6.

23. For example, his mural of Washington crossing the Delaware, at the Capitol Theater, Trenton, New Jersey, pictured in *American Magazine of Art* 17, no. 5 (May, 1926): 250.

24. Henry Clarence Pitz, "George Harding," *American Artist* 21, no. 10 (Dec., 1957): 30–31.

25. Exhibition catalog, in folder, "Harding, George," archives of the Pennsylvania Academy of the Fine Arts, Philadelphia. Early in the war years, Harding also mounted a show of eighteen of his works in tempera of Newfoundland scenes at the Corcoran Gallery, Washington, D.C., Feb. 21 to Mar. 12, 1942. See account in *Washington D.C. Star*, Mar. 1, 1942.

26. *Philadelphia Evening Bulletin*, Oct. 6, 1945. There are several photographs of Harding as a Marine Corps captain in folder, "Harding, George," in the archives of the Pennsylvania Academy of the Fine Arts. One of Harding's World War II paintings was reproduced in color in *Life*, Oct. 8, 1945.

27. "A Salute to the Marines," *Carnegie Magazine* 18, no. 8 (Jan., 1945): 242–44; *Philadelphia Inquirer*, Nov. 10, 1945. Other exhibits of Harding's World War II art were held at the Metropolitan Museum of Art in New York, and in museums in Sydney and Melbourne.

28. See Pitz, "George Harding," pp. 29–30; exhibition catalog, 1957, copy in folder, "Harding, George," archives, Pennsylvania Academy of the Fine Arts; *New York Times*, Apr. 27, 1945.

29. Harding's wife had died in 1953. Obituaries of Harding are in the *Philadelphia Inquirer* and the *Philadelphia Evening Bulletin*, Mar. 27, 1959.

30. Capt. Wallace Morgan, monthly report for Dec., 1918, to Chief, G-2D, Folder 5; GHQ, AEF, special orders no. 50, paragraph 98, to Capt. Wallace Morgan, Feb. 19, 1919.

31. "Wallace Morgan," *Etchings*.

32. Reed, *Illustrator in America*, p. 62; anon., "Wallace Morgan Story," pp. 2–3.

33. Frohman, "Wallace Morgan, Illustrator," p. 355.

34. Anon., "Wallace Morgan Story," pp. 13–17.

35. Ibid., p. 23, and Morgan's illustrations for an article by Lt. Col. Walter L. J. Bayler, "Last Man Off Wake Island," *Saturday Evening Post* 215, no. 40 (Apr. 3, 1943): 13.

36. Reed, *Illustrator in America*, p. 62. Like Duncan, Morgan never married.

37. Anon., "Wallace Morgan Story," p. 21. Regarding the camera, Morgan once stated that "the photograph of course is static and results in a lack of action, lack of humor, and lack of character and expression. Everything is static" (Watson, *Forty Illustrators and How They Work*, p. 210).

38. Peixotto, *American Front*, p. 207.

39. Peixotto's account of his German trip is in ibid., pp. 205–27.

40. Ibid., pp. 226–27.

41. Capt. Ernest Peixotto, monthly report for Dec., 1918, to Chief, G-2D, Folder 3.

42. U.S. Army, AEF, 1917–1919, Art Training Center, Bellevue, France, *Report of the American E.F. Art Training Center: Bellevue, Seine-et-Oise, March–June 1919* (Paris: Frazier-Soye, Imprimeur, 1919). See also GHQ, AEF, special orders no. 39, paragraph 51, Feb. 8, 1919, Folder 3, ordering Peixotto to report for duty at the art center.

43. Peixotto, "Report of the Department of Painting," in U.S. Army, *Report of the American E.F. Art Training Center*, pp. 59–60.

44. Memoranda, from Capt. Ernest Peixotto to Maj. Donald L. Stone, May 20, 1919; from Maj. Donald L. Stone to Capt. Ernest Peixotto, May 10, 1919; Capt. Ernest Peixotto, monthly report for Apr., 1919, to chief, G-2D; and Brig. Gen. D. E. Nolan, Army Chief of Staff, G-2, to the Honorable Joseph C. Grew, May 10, 1919, all in Folder 3.

45. For details, see "The Fontainebleau School of the Fine Arts," *American Magazine of Art* 14, no. 2 (Feb., 1923): 84–87. The French were aware of Peixotto's service in the cause of close Franco-American relations through art and decorated him as a Chevalier of the French Foreign Legion in 1921, elevating him to Officer in the Order in 1924.

46. Among Peixotto's postwar books were *Through Spain and Portugal* (1922) and *A Bacchic Pilgrimage: French Wines* (1932), both published by Scribner's.

47. Giles Edgerton, "Mural Decorations Appropriate for Modern Homes," *Arts and Decoration* 25 (May, 1926): 50–51; "Irish Landscape in a California House," *American Magazine of Art* 17, no. 4 (Apr., 1926): 195–97; "Arresting Murals of Classic Inspiration," *Arts and Decoration* 31 (Oct., 1929): 63; and *American Magazine of Art* 21, no. 4 (Apr., 1930): 236–37, for discussion of murals painted for the John C. Cravens home, Pasadena, California.

48. *New York Times*, Dec. 26, 1926, and Mar. 15, 1931; discussion of his bank murals in *American Magazine of Art* 19, no. 8 (Aug., 1928): 443, 452–53; and collection, "California Art Research," vol. IX, p. 52, Roll NDA/Cal 1, AAA/NPG.

49. *New York Times*, Dec. 7, 1940. Early in 1940, Peixotto was honored by a special dinner at the Hotel Brevoort, in New York City, which featured many testimonials and speeches, including one by Mayor La Guardia. See program and menu in folder, "Peixotto, Ernest," National Portrait Gallery library, Washington, D.C.

50. First endorsement to Smith's monthly report of Nov. 1, 1918, from Maj. A. L. James, Jr., to Capt. J. André Smith, Nov. 19, 1918; Capt. J. André Smith, monthly reports for Sept. through Dec., 1918, to Chief, G-2D, all in Folder 4. James was willing enough for the artists to maintain their studios in Paris but asked Smith to "keep in mind that they should be in the field as much as possible," spending time in Paris only "if actual need of their going to Paris for the completion of their work," existed.

51. Capt. J. André Smith, monthly report for Jan., 1919, to Chief, G-2D. There is a list of Smith's 194 drawings in numerical order of their submission with the brief title of each in Folder 4.

52. Capt. J. André Smith to Capt. Donald L. Stone, Feb. 15, 1919, Folder 4. (Capt. Joseph Mills Hanson had written a series of pieces in *Stars and Stripes* devoted to the histories of the American combat divisions and what they accomplished in the war.) Lt. Col. Aristides Moreno, then Acting Secretary, G-2, memorandum to Personnel Bureau, GHQ, AEF, Feb. 26, 1919, Folder 4.

53. Smith, *In France with the American Expeditionary Forces*, from the foreword, n.p.

54. See notice of an exhibition of some of Smith's etchings of Spain and southern France held at the galleries of Arthur H. Harlow and Company in New York City from Feb. 11 to Mar. 3, 1922 [Hahlo had changed the spelling of his name to Harlow]. See in frame 410, Roll N108, collection, "Prints Division, NYPL," AAA/NPG.

55. J. André Smith, *The Scenewright: The Making of Stage Models and Settings* (New York: Macmillan, 1926). See also his book: *Settings by Icon Bitchowski [pseud.]* (Pine Orchard, Conn.: n.p., n.d.). This book contains sketches of settings for the staging of *Romeo and Juliet, Hamlet, As You Like It, What Price Glory, My Old Kentucky Home*, and *The Merchant of Venice*.

56. Jeff Kunerth, "The Once and Future Dream of André Smith," in the *Florida Magazine*, supplement to the *Orlando Sentinel*, Apr. 3, 1983, p. 12.

57. For Smith's activities as artist in the late 1920s and early 1930s, see catalog for exhibition of etchings by André Smith from Apr. 7 to 28, 1928, at Harlow, McDonald and Company, in frames 411–15, Roll N108, collection, "Prints Division, NYPL," AAA/

NPG. See also Helen Fagg, "Etchers in America," *Fine Prints of the Year* (London: Halton and Truscott Smith, annual, 1928): 15–19; Susan A. Hutchinson, in "American Prints of the Year" (*Fine Prints of the Year* 11 [1933]: 18).

58. J. André Smith, *Art and the Subconscious: A Book of Drawings by André Smith* (Maitland, Fla.: The Research Studio, 1937).

59. "André Smith, 1880–1959," MPL, p. 4; and frames 416–17, Roll N108, collection, "Prints Division, NYPL," AAA/NPG. The Research Studio was sometimes referred to as "An Insanitorium of Art." See Smith's "An Insanitorium of Art," *Art Instruction* 3, no. 9 (Nov., 1939): 14–15, 28.

60. *The Maitland Art Center* (brochure), Maitland, Fla.

61. Kunerth, "The Once and Future Dream," p. 13.

62. Ibid., pp. 13–14. It is of interest that the American novelist Winston Churchill was once in residence along with the artists.

63. "André Smith, 1880–1959," MPL, pp. 7–8.

64. *Maitland Art Center* (brochure). The Maitland Art Center is said to be haunted by the ghost of Smith. See Dean Johnson and Laura Stewart, "Nice Place for a Haunting," *Florida Magazine,* supplement to the *Orlando Sentinel,* Oct. 28, 1984, pp. 11–13, 15–16.

65. Memoranda, from Capt. Harry E. Townsend to Chief, G-2D, Nov. 16, 1918, and first endorsement of this document, from GHQ, AEF, G-2D, Nov. 19, 1918; from Capt. Harry E. Townsend to Chief, G-2D, Dec. 9, 1918; Capt. Harry E. Townsend, combined monthly reports for Jan. and Feb., 1919, to Chief, G-2D; GHQ, AEF, special orders no. 9, paragraph 125, Jan. 9, 1919, all in Folder 2.

66. See portfolio, "World War I Sketches," Sanford Low Fund, 70.58.1-3 LIC, in Sanford Low Memorial Collection of American Art, New Britain Museum of American Art, New Britain, Conn.

67. Capt. Harry E. Townsend, combined monthly reports for Jan. and Feb. and monthly reports for Mar. and Apr., 1919, to Chief, G-2D; GHQ, AEF, special orders no. 60, paragraph 127, Mar. 1, 1919, all in Folder 2. The orders directed Townsend to proceed from Paris to Chaumont, Toul, Baccarat, St. Mihiel, and Montfaucon, on temporary assignment, to enable him to revisit the scenes of American action. For his sailing, see Brig. Gen. D. E. Nolan, memorandum to Personnel Bureau, GHQ, AEF, May 16, 1919; GHQ, AEF, special orders No. 137, paragraph 72, May 17, 1919; and Capt. Harry E. Townsend, monthly report for May, 1919, to Capt. Donald L. Stone, May 24, 1919, all in Folder 2. There is a copy of Townsend's discharge in "Portfolio of World War Sketches," 70.57.1-214 LIC.

68. *New Canaan Advertiser,* Aug. 23, 1934; and *Bridgeport Sunday Post,* Oct. 9, 1938. Some insights into Townsend's philosophy of art can be found in "Brothers in Art," *The Art Student* 1, no. 8 (Fall, 1916): 243–45. This was a publication of the Art Institute of Chicago, and the article consisted of a letter from Harry to his brother Lee Townsend, then a student at the Institute. An appraisal of his work in the AEF is in Walt Reed, "Harry Townsend: On Assignment during World War I," *American Artist* 36, no. 358 (May, 1972): 62–67, 86–87. This article includes examples of Townsend's combat art.

69. *Norwalk Hour,* July 30, 1941.

Chapter 5

1. Gen. Peyton C. March, Chief of Staff, for the Adjutant General of the Army, memorandum for transmission via cablegram to Pershing in France, undated [June, 1919], folder, "Dunn reference," SDMAC. The cablegram stated that "five returned artists have been discharged. It is not desired that any of those remaining be held in service to complete work."

2. Maj. Gen. W. G. Haan, memorandum to the Chief of Staff, Washington, D.C., July, 1919, in folder, "Dunn reference," SDMAC.

3. W. de C. Ravenel to Prof. W. H. Holmes, Director, National Gallery of Art, Smithsonian Institution, July 19, 1919, in file, "Accession No. 64592, Office of the Registrar," Smithsonian Institution, Washington, D.C. (cited hereafter as file, "Accession No. 64592.") See letter of acceptance from W. de C. Ravenel to Col. C. W. Weeks, Washington, D.C., July 19, 1919, and other relevant letters in this file.

4. See catalog in file "Accession No. 64592."

5. Only Aylward's work, for unknown reasons, was excluded from this exhibition.

6. S. L. A. Marshall, *American Heritage History of World War I* (New York: American Heritage Publishing Company, 1964), and "A War Portfolio of American Artists," *American Heritage* 10, no. 6 (Oct., 1959): 7–17.

Index

Art from the Trenches was composed into type on a compugraphic digital photo-typesetter in eleven point Trump Medieval with four points of spacing between the lines. Trump was also selected for display. The book was designed by Jim Billingsley, typeset by Metricomp, Inc., printed offset by Thomson-Shore, Inc., and bound by John H. Dekker & Sons, Inc. The paper on which this book is printed carries acid-free characteristics for an effective life of at least three hundred years.

TEXAS A&M UNIVERSITY PRESS : COLLEGE STATION